D1478112

your stress-free
wedding planner

experts' best secrets to creating
the wedding of your dreams

judy allen

SOURCEBOOKS CASABLANCA™
AN IMPRINT OF SOURCEBOOKS, INC.®
NAPERVILLE, ILLINOIS

DISCARDED

Copyright © 2004 by Judy Allen
Cover and internal design © 2004 by Sourcebooks, Inc.
Cover illustration by Megan Dempster
Sourcebooks and the colophon are registered trademarks of Sourcebooks, Inc.

All rights reserved. No part of this book may be reproduced in any form or by any electronic or mechanical means including information storage and retrieval systems—except in the case of brief quotations embodied in critical articles or reviews—without permission in writing from its publisher, Sourcebooks, Inc.

Published by Sourcebooks, Inc.
P.O. Box 4410, Naperville, Illinois 60567-4410
(630) 961-3900
FAX: (630) 961-2168
www.sourcebooks.com

Library of Congress Cataloging-In-Publication Data
Allen, Judy, 1952-
   Your stress-free wedding planner : experts' best secrets to creating the wedding of your dreams / by Judy Allen.
      p. cm.
   ISBN 1-4022-0297-0 (alk. paper)
   1. Weddings—Planning. 2. Wedding etiquette. I. Title.
HQ745.A35 2004
395.2'2—dc22
                                        2004013840

Printed and bound in China
PP 10 9 8 7 6 5 4 3 2 1

Contents

Congratulations on Your Engagement v

How to Use Your Wedding Planner: 10 Effortless Steps to Your Dream Wedding vii

Section One: Designing Your Wedding

Step 1: Excited but Calm: Visualize Your Wedding Day Dreams 1

    Visualizing Your Wedding Day Dreams

    Creating Your Wedding Vision

    Wedding Vision Questionnaire

Step 2: Focusing on What Matters Most: Making the Important Decisions First 19

    Decision Making

    Guest List Worksheet

    Our Shared Wedding Vision Worksheet

Step 3: It's All under Control: Designing Your Realistic Blueprint 39

    Creating Your Wedding Blueprint

    Wedding Day Blueprint

Section Two: Planning Your Wedding

Step 4: When It's Perfect, It's Easy: Choosing the Perfect
          Wedding and Reception Site 49

    Finding the Perfect Site for Your Wedding Ceremony and Reception

    Wedding Ceremony and Reception Requirements Questionnaire

    What Your Proposed Venue Will Need to Know

    Questionnaire for Each Venue

Step 5: Taking Good Care of You: Selecting the Right Wedding Vendors 73

    Supplier's Information Worksheet

    Questions to Ask Prospective Suppliers

    Invitations and Other Print Material

    Transportation

    Décor

    Floral Arrangements

    Centerpieces

    Food

    Beverages

Rentals

Music and Entertainment

Audiovisual, Staging, and Lighting

Photography

Finishing Touches

Get It in Writing

Quick Overview of Possible Wedding Event Elements and Price Considerations

Miscellaneous

Step 6: Staying Centered About Finances: What to Ask
       Before You Sign on the Dotted Line. 127
Cost and Contract Negotiations

Section Three: Coordinating Your Wedding

Step 7: Planning for Ease: Creating Your Critical Path 141
Charting Your Critical Path

Wedding Critical Path Worksheet

Step 8: Go with the Flow: Flow Sheets Make Your Wedding Day
       Flawless and Relaxed 153
Wedding Day Contact Information

Wedding Venue and Supplier Contact Sheet

Wedding Schedule of Events

Wedding Flow Sheets

Step 9: Stress-Free All the Way to the Big Moment: Wedding Supplier
       Previews and Wedding Day Rehearsal 167

Step 10: Like Clockwork: On-Site Wedding Day Orchestration 171
After the Wedding

Conclusion

Wedding Planning Forms and Checklists 175

Index 213

About the Author 216

Congratulations On Your Engagement

YOUR JOURNEY TO life as a married couple begins with the first rush of excitement of sharing the news, followed by engagement celebrations where talk quickly turns to wedding plans. In a matter of moments, you can move from newly engaged to having a wedding to plan, and this is where you need to proceed with care.

Stepping into wedding planning mode too soon can initially feel overwhelming and create a false sense of urgency. You'll quickly come to find that everyone has an opinion—family, friends, loved ones, co-workers, and even complete strangers are all eager to contribute their well-meaning thoughts, ideas, and recommendations.

Every bridal couple wants a perfect wedding day—one that is meaningful, memorable, and magical. It is important that this day capture everything that has special meaning to each of you. To be able to do this, you need to have a clear vision of what you both want.

Once you have your wedding design firmly in place, one that is perfect for both of you, then it is easy to bring others in, listen to their thoughts, and be open to suggestions and ideas that may complement your wedding plans. You will know immediately if a thought has merit and is worth pursuing or if it's not for you and does not fit in with your wedding vision. You'll find it easy to make decisions, avoid conflict, find areas of creative compromise, and come to discover that wedding planning is not an ordeal to get through, but a joyful experience you will long remember. It begins with a vision and ten effortless steps that will show you how to create the wedding of your dreams—stress free.

How To Use Your Wedding Planner

10 Effortless Steps to Your Dream Wedding

EVERY WEDDING MOVES through the same series of planning steps, but the time, money, energy, and emotion invested can vary tremendously. I have designed ten simple—but very specific—steps that I have used to create, produce, and orchestrate special events around the world in over thirty countries, for up to two thousand guests. This method produces successful events with ease, including the biggest event most people plan in their lives—their wedding.

These ten steps, which are outlined in detail in this wedding planner, will walk you through the event-planning principles and include lists of questions, checklists, and forms that professional bridal consultants and event planners use when planning a special occasion.

These same ten steps of event planning apply whether your wedding is large or small; being held locally, out of state, or out of country; regardless of the budget; the choice of venue; whether it is being held inside or outside; on land or on sea; taking place during the day or in the evening; and being held in the spring, summer, fall, or winter.

Each step will guide you to the next. As you move through the ten steps, you will find that you are building the knowledge that is necessary to move your plans forward and enable you to make informed decisions about your wedding day. Because you will always know exactly where you stand, know what to expect, what to look for, what to look out for, what you have spent, what still needs to be done, when it needs to be done by, and how to best organize it, there will be no last-minute mad dash that will leave you feeling frazzled instead of being full of anticipation. Planning your wedding in these ten steps becomes stress free and leaves you feeling in complete control of your wedding plans.

The order that the planning steps are laid out is one of the keys to a successful day. In order to produce the best possible result, they must be followed in sequence. Each step is broken down further into small, manageable tasks. At no time will you feel overwhelmed or unsure. All the tips, techniques, and tools you will need to plan your special day are in your planner.

Your planner is divided into three specific sections: Designing Your Wedding, Planning Your Wedding, and Coordinating Your Wedding. Steps 1, 2, and 3 focus on wedding design. You will be guided through the process of visualization and decision making. You will also be shown how to create a wedding day blueprint that is tailormade to fit you as a couple, fulfill your dreams, be respectful to both your families, incorporate personal touches and traditions, and come well within your wedding budget.

Steps 4, 5, and 6, explain how to find the perfect venue for your wedding and reception, where to go to find exactly what you need, expert tips on contract negotiations, and what you need to know before you sign on the dotted line and commit to your suppliers.

How to arrive at your wedding day heady with anticipation, relaxed, and confident that your wedding day will be as meaningful, memorable, and magical as you always envisioned it would be, is laid out in Steps 7, 8, 9, and 10.

Excited but Calm

Visualize Your Wedding Day Dreams

MANY BRIDES-TO-BE create their initial wedding day vision long before they have met their intended. This may or may not necessarily be the case with all grooms-to-be. This is your time to fantasize. Working together, as you start to plan your wedding day, a new vision will be created.

What is important is to discover how you both saw this very special day happening in your minds. Are you surrounded by loving family members and friends? Are there just the two of you on a windswept beach at sunrise, on a mountaintop, or by a waterfall in Hawaii? Perhaps your dream wedding is a small gathering of the very special people in your life in a backyard garden setting? When you dance your first dance together as a couple, is there a band playing in the background or a classical guitarist? What is important to discover at the very beginning is whether you both share the same dream wedding day or if they seemingly go in opposite directions. Don't worry if you find you diverge quite a bit—by the end of this process, I promise you'll both be happy!

Once your wedding day dreams have been laid out, it will be very easy to discover the common elements you are both looking for and identify the feeling or emotion you both want to bring to your wedding. This is truly where your wedding design process begins. Once you know the emotion that will be the design force in creating your wedding day, you can begin to look at how it can be best accomplished.

Visualizing Your Wedding Day Dreams

THERE ARE FIVE important areas to consider when visualizing your wedding. They are:

- 🎋 The Elements—All the Parts That Make Up Your Wedding
- 🎋 The Essentials—Must-Haves
- 🎋 The Environment—Wedding Day Venue and Style
- 🎋 The Energy—Creating a Mood
- 🎋 The Emotion—Feelings

The Elements—All the Parts That Make Up Your Wedding

The first step when planning any event is to look at the big picture. Step back and take an overview look at the events that could be taking place in your life the days just before your wedding, on your actual wedding day, and on the days immediately following. The best way to do this is to lay everything out on a Wedding Flow overview worksheet that focuses on the week your wedding takes place. This exercise takes place before you finalize your wedding date and even before you begin to look at ceremony venues and reception sites. Your Wedding Flow worksheet will end up providing you with valuable insight about your budgeting, wedding day timing, logistics, and orchestration, which could impact your final choices. It is a useful event planning tool that will evolve as your wedding unfolds and is the foundation upon which all your wedding elements will be built.

There are usually three main components that couples planning their wedding focus on:

1. the rehearsal and rehearsal dinner;
2. the ceremony; and
3. the reception.

But there is so much more to take into consideration in order to produce a picture-perfect wedding day—one that flows seamlessly and effortlessly. Consideration must be given to the timing, logistics, and orchestration of all the wedding day elements that lead up to your actual event, your wedding day, and the immediate days following your event that can include:

- 🎋 Wedding attire final fittings
- 🎋 Makeup and hair rehearsal
- 🎋 Marriage license picked up

- Wedding rings picked up
- Early arrival of out-of-town guests
- Pre-wedding guest entertainment
- Bachelor/bachelorette party
- Wedding rehearsal
- Rehearsal dinner
- Advance move-in and setup of the ceremony venue
- Advance move-in and setup of the reception venue
- Bride and groom transportation to the ceremony, photographs, the reception, and onward
- Wedding party transportation to the ceremony, photographs, the reception, and return
- Wedding ceremony
- Wedding photos
- Wedding reception
- Wedding night
- Honeymoon
- Teardown and move-out of wedding ceremony venue
- Teardown and move-out of the wedding reception venue

Make a copy of the Wedding Flow Overview Worksheet in the forms and checklists section of this book. Begin to pencil in under the appropriate days the schedule of event elements—your wedding flow—as you are visualizing them now. At this point, you are not working with actual timing and logistics, just an overview of how you see your wedding week unfolding.

After you fill in the Wedding Flow Overview Worksheet, read through the rest of this chapter, and complete Our Wedding Vision Questionnaire at the end. Make extra copies so that you can play with your initial wedding elements, arranging them in a variety of ways to see which is the best fit for your special event. Always make sure to keep a blank master copy. Please be sure to work in pencil, as you will want to make adjustments as you move forward.

The Essentials—Must-Haves

If you're like many couples today, you're throwing away the book of wedding day "shoulds." When it comes to wedding etiquette, there are no more rules. Couples like you are opting instead to do what feels right to you; is aligned with your religious and personal beliefs, traditions, and customs; and resonates with who you are.

Wedding "must-haves" are what matter most to both of you. They are determined by:

- What will be meaningful to you as an individual and as a couple
- What will make your wedding day memorable to you both
- What will capture the magic of your relationship

Your wedding day must-haves are not based on dollars and cents, but on emotional currency and how they touch your senses. For one groom, proud of his Scottish heritage and wanting to honor his deceased parents, his wedding day must-have was being married wearing a kilt. It mattered greatly to him and, because it did, it mattered greatly to his bride, who was not Scottish, but Jewish. Theirs was an interfaith and intercultural wedding. And it was her suggestion—not his—to have a bagpiper pipe the wedding party in. It was a wedding gift she could give to him that was meaningful, made their wedding memorable, and captured the giving nature of their relationship.

One bride and groom, who met in a donut shop, decided that one of their wedding must-haves would embrace the memory of that special day. Instead of a traditional wedding cake, they had one made from Krispy Kreme Doughnuts. A standard wedding cake would just not have had as much meaning to them and their guests were captivated by their imaginative flair.

For some couples, a wedding day must-have is one that is steeped in cultural or religious tradition or ceremony. For others, their must-haves may be personal to them or part of their family heritage.

Some must-haves are easy to include, while others require more thought, planning, and money. It is important to learn both of your must-haves as you begin to visualize your wedding. Remember to think each decision through in terms of emotional currency, in meeting a wedding need and not a wedding want. Both your must-haves will become the core of your wedding design and your wedding elements will naturally begin to unfold around them.

The Environment—Wedding Day Venue and Style

Today the venues for wedding ceremonies and receptions are limited only by the bridal couple's imagination. Marriages today take place on land, on water, underwater (scuba diving), midair (skydiving or onboard aircraft), or sitting on top of the world in a Ferris wheel!

Some couples prefer to exchange their wedding vows and have their reception in the same spot. Others prefer to be married in one location and hold the reception in another venue.

Wedding Day Venue

Your initial vision and where you ultimately hold your ceremony and wedding reception can end up being worlds apart. When looking for a place to hold your ceremony and reception—traditional or unique—you will need to consider some key points.

Location

Who you want to attend your wedding will play a factor in deciding your wedding ceremony and reception location. Where do most of your guests live? If they do not live in your area, what are the realistic possibilities of them being able to attend your wedding? For some guests, no matter how much they would love to be with you on your special day, depending on their personal financial and family situation it just may not be an option. Some couples who have moved away from home, out of country, or out of state, decide to go back home for their wedding as opposed to holding it in a location that would limit attendance of beloved family members. They hold a wedding celebration party when they return for close friends who might not have been able to attend.

Date

If you have selected a date over a long weekend, take into consideration that costs can be higher, and be prepared to ask about these things when you begin to look at venues. Union labor costs at a hotel, for example, can be doubled or you may be required to pay catering staff, bartenders, or waitstaff a higher rate for working over a holiday. If there are last-minute problems, you need to know whether key support people will be in place or whether the establishment will be running on a skeleton staff.

Season

Seasons play a part in venue selection. (Step 4 is all about selecting your venue.) The same venue in different seasons can produce a different set of wedding logistical and budget considerations. Every season can have its own challenges, depending on the type of venue you choose. For example, a tented wedding taking place in the height of summer during the heat of the day would require the cost of air-conditioning, back-up generators, or ceiling fans. A heating system or free-standing heaters, flooring, and lighting would be factors for a tented wedding held in early spring or late fall when it is considerably cooler and it gets dark much earlier. The same applies to building sites. One bride collapsed in a quaint chapel that did not have air-conditioning due to the heat and the weight of her wedding dress, which was too heavy in the scorching heat.

Time of day

Time of day is an important factor. Will you be the only bridal couple getting married or holding your reception in the venue or will multiple weddings be scheduled? If multiple weddings or receptions are being held, will you feel as though you are in an assembly line? What happens if the wedding or reception that takes place before yours gets a late start? What is the turnaround time for your suppliers to set up and your guests to have access to go into the room? What happens if their guests linger? Or, if you are the ones holding the earlier time slot, how will you handle making sure that guests depart on time so that the next bridal couple can set up? Will you feel rushed or harried, and are you better served holding your wedding ceremony and reception in a venue where you will be the only couple using the room on the day you have selected?

Whether you are planning an indoor or outdoor affair

If you plan for an outdoor wedding, you will need to have a bad weather backup. For spring, summer, and fall weddings, this can be a tent or a private room at the same facility that has been reserved for you in case of inclement weather. Outdoor events also require special setup and cost considerations. For example, if you are setting up a tent, depending on your requirements, move-in and setup can take anywhere from two to three days to a week and set up could be delayed if it rains and time also has to be factored in for the ground to dry. Teardown and move-out can take a couple of days as well. Depending on where you are holding your event, you may have to factor in site rental charges for setup and teardown days as well as the facility not being able to rent that space to anyone else over that time period. You would also have to check labor costs for teardown on a Sunday to see if there would be any additional charges. Other cost factors could include having the grounds cared for or separate cooking tents for the caterers if the venue does not have a kitchen available or one that will meet your needs and security.

Whether the wedding ceremony and reception are taking place in the same venue or two separate facilities

If you are holding your wedding ceremony and reception in two different facilities, you need to give thought to the travel time between the two venues, if your guests can easily travel between the two locations, where you will be having your photographs done, what your guests will be doing in the interim, and how you want to stage your arrival.

If the wedding ceremony and reception are taking place under one roof, will you be departing after the ceremony to have photographs taken at another spot or will all pictures be taken at the site? Will there be any time lag between the wedding ceremony and the start of the reception? What do you have planned for the guests while they are waiting for the bridal party to return to the reception from having their pictures taken?

Budget considerations

Not all venues are created equal concerning their terms and conditions. For example, what is included at no additional cost in a hotel (tables, chairs, linens, specialty glasses such as martini glasses for a martini bar) is not necessarily included in the room rental cost in a convention center, wedding hall, museum, etc.

Wedding Day Style

Your wedding style is the atmosphere or overall effect you are trying to achieve. Styles can be mixed and matched to create something new that represents you as a couple. Style is personalized. There are no "shoulds" in style and style is never about money. If your chosen wedding style or theme, for example, is romance, you can have an incredibly romantic wedding spending hundreds of dollars, thousands of dollars, or hundreds of thousands of dollars. What you have to spend may limit your options, but never the overlying theme or essence of your wedding day. Your wedding style will influence your choice of invitations, venue, bridal and attendants' attire, flowers, décor, music, entertainment, food, and beverages. Your end result will be layers of ambiance flowing together to create your wedding look or wedding style.

The Energy—Creating a Mood

The venue, décor, music, food and drink, activities, and the guest mix all contribute to the energy in the room and the mood that is being set. The energy you bring to your wedding ceremony and reception as a result of your wedding design can be good or bad. Poor design planning with regard to timing, logistical layout, and event elements can literally drain the energy from a room. This is the feeling you experience when things go flat, there is dead air, stilted conversation, awkward silences, and the room becomes devoid of energy. Negative energy can fill a room when there are overlooked areas of congestion, long waits, guests are hungry or tired, and there is insufficient seating. Choosing a room or a setting that is too big or too small for the size of the guest count can also bring down the energy in a room.

The Emotion—Feelings

The wedding style you select will lend itself to conveying the emotion surrounding your special day. For example, a romantic style may evoke feelings of tenderness, softness, intimacy, all wrapped up in love. A wedding ceremony and reception that has a fun theme, depicting the playful nature of the bride and groom will give off lighthearted warmth that is caring and affectionate. Give thought to your wedding style and the feelings that you want to bring out. Choose one that will capture the spirit of your relationship and the emotions that will make your wedding special.

Creating Your Wedding Vision

THE FOLLOWING QUESTIONS will help you to create your wedding day vision, help in determining which areas are most important to each of you, and guide you through budget considerations that you both will need to reflect on. Seemingly inconsequential items can quickly add up to hundreds and even thousands of dollars in unexpected costs if not factored into the very beginning stages of designing your wedding.

It is important that both of you take time to consider the questions and write down your responses. Make a copy of this form for each person to fill out. It is important for each person to complete this form independently, so as not to influence each other's answers. Once you have both completed your Wedding Vision Questionnaire, it is time to compare your thoughts and dreams to see if they are in sync, totally different, contain ideas that hold great appeal that you may not have considered before, or areas where event elements can be blended to create something new. It is a time of reflection, give and take, and compromise as you come together to create a vision you both will love and cherish in the years to come.

The questionnaire opens the door to discussion which will lead you into Step 2—decision making and determining what matters most to you and how it all fits into your wedding budget. You now have a base to begin to develop a design for a wedding day that is unique to you as a couple, custom created to be a true celebration of your love. This is your day and it is important to make it truly your own.

Make two copies of this form—one for the bride, one for the groom.

Wedding Date

- In what year do I see our wedding taking place? _____
- During what time of year (season) do I visualize our wedding being held? _____
- How much wedding planning time will that give me? _____
- What day of the week do I want our wedding to take place on? _____
- What time of day do I prefer to be married at? _____
- Is there a special date that is significant to me that I want to be married on or any date that I want to avoid? _____
- Will the time of year, month, date, or time affect attendance of close family members and friends that I want to be with me on our special day? _____
- Where (location, not venue) will our wedding ceremony ideally take place? _____
_____

Check any critical dates that may be taking place around your selected wedding date, such as major personal, family, or friend events (graduation, birth due date of a baby, special anniversary, birthday celebrations, national or religious holidays, or long weekends that could affect supplier delivery and guest attendance).

Bride's Family

- What immediate family members will be part of our wedding ceremony? _____
_____

Groom's Family

- What immediate family members will be part of our wedding ceremony? _____
_____

Wedding Party

- Who will be walking me/us down the aisle? _____
- How many people in total will be in our wedding party? _____
  - Maid/Matron of Honor _____
  - Bridal Attendants _____
  - Best Man _____
  - Groomsmen _____
- Will we be having a:
  - Flower Girl? _____

Ring Bearer? _____

Ushers? _____

• Will the members of the wedding party be invited to bring a guest? _____

Wedding Guests

• Do I prefer a large or small wedding? _____

• How many guests do I visualize attending? _____

• Will single guests be invited to bring a guest? _____

• What is the age range of the guests we will be inviting? _____

• Do I see children being invited to our wedding? _____

• Will any guests have any special needs, such as handicap accessibility? _____

• Will any of the guests have to come in from another town, state, or country? _____

• Will we be required to host or entertain out-of-town guests? _____

Invitations

• Am I open to invitation styles or do I have something particular in mind? _____

Wedding Ceremony

• Where do I see our wedding ceremony taking place and our vows being exchanged?

_____

• Is the wedding ceremony taking place inside or outside? _____

• Do I see our wedding ceremony being a formal or informal event? _____

• What do I see the wedding party wearing? _____

• Where is the wedding ceremony location in relationship to where we live? _____

_____

• Where is the wedding ceremony location in relationship to where our guests live?

_____

• Will a bridal suite be required at the wedding ceremony location for the bride, groom, or any other members of the bridal party to dress in? _____

Wedding Ceremony Décor

• As the guests are arriving at the wedding ceremony, what do I envision they will see from the moment that they arrive until they are seated? _____

• How do I envision the wedding ceremony stage to look? _____

• What are my favorite flowers? _____

• What flowers hold special meaning for me? _____

• What flowers hold special meaning for us as a couple? _____
• What is my favorite color? _____
• What wedding color scheme am I initially drawn to? _____

Wedding Ceremony Music

• What do I imagine our wedding guests will be listening to while they wait for the bridal party to arrive? _____
• What type of music will be playing as the bridal procession begins? _____
• What song will signal the arrival of the bride? _____
• Will live musical performances be a part of our wedding processional or ceremony?

_____

Wedding Ceremony Lighting

• What ambience does the lighting project? _____
• What mood do I want the room to convey? _____
• How will the wedding ceremony stage be lit? _____

Wedding Party Arrival

• How do I see the wedding party arriving at the ceremony? Will they be making their own way there, have drivers assigned to them, or arrive by limousine or some other transportation mode? _____
• What transportation do I envision for the bride and the groom to the ceremony? _____
• Where will we be coming from (e.g., parents' home, friend's home, hotel, or other location)?

_____

• Who will be accompanying each of us? _____

Wedding Photographs at the Ceremony

• Will we be having professional wedding photographs, videos, or a live wedding webcast of our ceremony? _____
• Who will be taking wedding photographs, videos, or wedding webcast? _____

_____

Wedding Vows

• What is of utmost importance to me to have in our wedding ceremony? _____
• Who do I see conducting the wedding ceremony? _____

- Do I see us exchanging traditional wedding vows, vows tailored to us, or vows written by us? _____
- Are there any special family, cultural, or religious traditions that would be very meaningful to me or to us to include? _____
- How do I see the wedding processional unfolding? _____
  _____
- How long do I see the wedding ceremony taking from beginning to end? _____
- After we are joined in matrimony and are exiting the wedding stage, what do I see taking place? _____
- What music will be played as we are introduced to our guests and walk back down the aisle as husband and wife? _____

Wedding Photographs Before or After the Ceremony
- Will I want family photographs taken before or after the ceremony? _____
- What backdrop will I want to see in my wedding photographs? _____
- How will the wedding party be transported to the photograph location and wedding reception?
  _____

Wedding Reception Venue
- Will I want the wedding ceremony and wedding reception to take place in the same location?
  _____
- If our reception is being held in a secondary location, will it present any transportation concerns for our guests? _____
- Where do I see our wedding reception taking place? _____
- What type of venue would best suit our wedding reception? _____
- Do I see the wedding reception taking place inside or outside? _____
- Do I see our wedding reception being a formal or informal event? _____

Wedding Reception Arrival
- Do I see the guests arriving at the venue in advance of the wedding party (e.g., while photographs are being taken)? _____
- What do I have in mind for the guests to do in the interim (e.g., will there be refreshments and entertainment)? _____
- Will we need a separate area in which to host the arrival and then move the guests into another room once the wedding party arrives? _____
- Will seating be required for any or all of the guests? _____

- Will we have a receiving line? _____
- How do I see our reception unfolding? _____
  _____
- How long do I see our reception going on? _____

Wedding Reception Room Requirements

- How do I see the room being laid out? _____
- Will it be a stand-up reception with scattered seating? _____
- Will it be a sit-down affair with table seating for all guests? _____
- If we are including dinner, will seating be open or will we having set seating and a seating chart? _____
- Will there be food stations or buffet setups or will food be passed or plated? _____
- Will there be bars set up in the room or will beverages be served by waitstaff? _____
- Where will the wedding party be seated? _____
- Where will the wedding cake be positioned? _____
- Will a stage be required for speeches, the musicians, DJ, or entertainment? _____
- Will there be dancing? _____
- Will there be any audiovisual requirements such as rear screen projection, plasma screens, etc., which need to be factored into the room size requirements? _____
  _____

Wedding Reception Décor

- As the guests are arriving at the wedding reception, what do I envision they will see as they arrive? _____
- What type of décor do I see in the room? _____
- How do I see the room being set? Table settings? Centerpieces? Flowers? Colors? What do I see in the room? _____
  _____

Wedding Reception Entertainment

- Will we have a DJ, live musicians, a dance band, or piped-in background music? _____
  _____
- What type of music will be played? _____
- What song do I see us dancing our first dance to? _____
- Who will be our MC? _____

Wedding Reception Lighting

• How do I see the room being lit? _____

Wedding Reception Audiovisual

• Will there be speeches or toasts? _____

• Will a podium or microphones be required? _____

• Will we have any audiovisual requirements? _____

Wedding Reception Food and Beverage

• What type of beverages will we be serving? _____

• Will it be a hosted bar or cash bar? _____

• Will we provide champagne or any other beverage for toasting? _____

• What type of food do I see being served at our wedding reception? _____

Bridal Couple Departure

• Will there be any special fanfare as we depart? _____

• Where do I see us spending our first night together? _____

• How will we be transported from the wedding reception? _____

Pre-Wedding Events

• Is a "traditional" bachelor/bachelorette party something that we will consider attending, or would it cause conflict? Will we be open to having a destination or joint bachelor/bachelorette party instead? _____

Wedding Rehearsal

• Will we be holding a wedding dress rehearsal? _____

• Will a rehearsal dinner be a part of our plans? _____

• Do I see it as being casual or formal? _____

• What will be the ideal location in which to hold our rehearsal dinner? ____

• Who will be included in the rehearsal dinner (e.g., just the wedding party or will out-of-town guests be open to attending as well)? _____

Bride's Attire Considerations

• What style of wedding dress will I be wearing, and will I be buying, borrowing, or renting it?

_____

- Will I be wearing a wedding veil? If so, will I be buying, borrowing, or renting it?

  _____

- Will I be wearing a headpiece? If so, will I be buying, borrowing, or renting it?

  _____

- What jewelry that I own will I be wearing? _____

- What jewelry will I need to buy or borrow to complete my wedding look? _____

  _____

- Will I be having my hair professionally done? _____

- Will I be having my makeup professionally done or purchase any? _____

- Will I be getting a professional manicure and pedicure? _____

- Will I need to buy special bridal shoes for the ceremony? _____

- What special lingerie will I be required to buy? _____

- What will be my something old? _____

- What will be my something new? _____

- What will be my something borrowed? _____

- What will be my something blue? _____

- Will my wedding ring need to be purchased? _____

- Will I be wearing gloves? If so, short or long? _____

- Will I need to purchase a small purse? _____

- Will I need to buy a garter? _____

- Will I be purchasing a special perfume for my wedding day? _____

- Will I need to pull together a mini personal care pouch filled with essential wedding day items for the bride, groom, and wedding party that one of my bridal attendants will carry throughout the day? _____

- Will I need a special going-away ensemble? _____

- Will I need to buy special going-away shoes? _____

- Will I need to buy going-away accessories? _____

Groom's Attire Considerations

- Will I be wearing a formal tuxedo, morning suit, or dress suit? _____

- Will I be renting, buying, or do I own my wedding clothing? _____

- Will I be renting, buying, or do I own proper dress shoes? _____

- What personal clothing items will I need to buy? _____

- Will I be purchasing a wedding band? _____

- What grooming aids will I require? _____

- Will I be having any professional grooming services done? _____

• What jewelry do I own that I will I be wearing (e.g., cuff links, tie pin, watch, etc.)?

_____

• Will I need to purchase special cologne? _____

• Will I need to buy going-away apparel? _____
• Will I need to buy going-away accessories? _____

Wedding Party Attire Considerations

• Will we be paying—in full or in part—for the wedding party attire, or will they be paying for all their own expenses? _____

• Will being a part of wedding party—if we are not paying all expenses—be a financial hardship for anyone? Are we putting anyone in a tight situation? _____

• Will we be giving gifts to all members of the wedding party? _____

Honeymoon Considerations

• Will we be going on a honeymoon immediately after the wedding, the next day, or later?

_____

• What will be the perfect honeymoon destination for us? _____
• How long will we be away, ideally? _____
• Do we know how much money we need to set aside for our honeymoon and expenses while we are away? _____

Other Wedding Budget Considerations

• Will we be holding any pre-wedding events for out-of-town guests? _____
• Will we need to budget for bringing in special family members, wedding party, or guests to our wedding who may not be able to attend otherwise? _____

• Do we know if our families will be contributing to our wedding? Will this cause financial hardship for anyone? Are we putting anyone in a tight situation if we accept his or her offer?

_____

• If our families are contributing to our wedding costs, do we know what dollars they will be providing (these are the budget parameters we need to be respectful of to ensure that there are no financial hardships incurred)? _____

• If our families are helping us with wedding expenses, will the money be given as a gift for us to use towards our total costs or will it come with concessions that need to be made that could change how we see our wedding day unfolding? _____

_____

• In exchange for family financial assistance, are we prepared to compromise what may be important to us as a couple (if the money given is not strictly a gift to help with wedding costs but comes with certain conditions attached)? _____

• What is our personal spending budget? If we are paying for the wedding on our own or paying for all expenses over and above what our families are contributing, what can we afford to spend without putting ourselves in debt or at financial risk? _____
_____

• Is what we are planning to do financially feasible given our preferred wedding date?
_____

Focusing on What Matters Most

Making the Important Decisions First

TAKE TIME NOW to sit and discuss your completed personal wedding visions. Shortly, you will be in a position to create a new wedding vision that incorporates both your wedding dreams. First, it is necessary to read through the material in Step 2, which will help you to make some key decisions and discover what is most meaningful. This is where "my" wedding vision becomes "our" wedding vision and clutter is swept away.

Decision Making

PLANNING YOUR WEDDING respectfully and responsibly, in regards to staying within your budget guidelines, will require serious decision making on your part. The key will be making sure what matters most to both of you is part of your wedding day—your wedding day essentials. All the rest are really just event elements—wedding day enhancements—that add extra touches to your wedding, but are really not essential. If you can include them, wonderful. If not, not having them there takes nothing away from your day or makes it any less perfect. What is important is maximizing the money you do have to spend, finding areas of creative compromise, and remaining open to new ideas that will bring about the end result you are looking for.

Deciding What Matters Most

There are four main areas that will have the most impact on your budget. The rest are secondary expenses. The four areas that most affect your costs are:

- ✂ Guest list
- ✂ Wedding venues
- ✂ Wedding reception styles
- ✂ Wedding reception inclusions

Guest List

Determining whether your wedding day is about the quantity of guests you will be inviting or the quality of the guests who will be coming will aid in decision making when you are considering the guest list. A wedding is a celebration of two lives joining together, and a time when most brides and grooms desire to be surrounded by family and close friends. Yet at some weddings, there are guests in attendance who have no real personal connection to either the bride or the groom—they are there as a family obligation or concession—and others who are business acquaintances and could be out of your life in a matter of days, weeks, or months. Keep your guest list in proper perspective.

Guest List Considerations

As you begin to consider who you will be inviting to your wedding, keep in mind what you have experienced at other family events, weddings, and social gatherings. Do you enjoy a get-together more when the room is packed with people, alive, and energized, or when the party is starting to die down, only close friends and family members remain, and there is a feeling of warmth and intimacy? Think about the energy and the emotion you want in the room with you, which entertaining style suits you as a couple, and choose your guest list carefully as it will play a big part in your venue selection and your wedding day inclusions.

Another guest list consideration is whether or not you will have an A and a B list of possible invitees. You may have decided that 50, 100, 250, or more is the maximum number of guests you will be inviting and plan your guest list accordingly. What you need to keep in mind is what happens if some guests will be unable to attend. Will you have others waiting in the wings who you would have liked to have included originally but couldn't due to already being at maximum numbers? If so, you need to pay special attention to when you send out your invitations and to the date you put on your RSVP cards.

Many wedding etiquette books suggest sending your invitations out at least eight weeks before your wedding, no later than six, and with an RSVP date two weeks before your wedding. Sending invitations out at least six to eight weeks before a society event or an at-home event is standard, but following that rule of thumb for a wedding can create time crunches.

An important consideration in determining the date to send out your invitations and request your RSVPs back is the date when you can reduce your guest numbers without paying higher cancellation penalties. Consider giving yourself an RSVP buffer of four to six weeks. This will allow you to send out a replacement invitation, if necessary, and handle any needed changes to food, beverage, and rental guarantees before you are down to the wire. If you are inviting family and close friends, they know that a wedding will be taking place and should have no problem sending in their RSVPs at a time that is right for you. You can go to the expense of sending out "save the date" cards or do a fun announcement to let people know that an invitation is coming, but some couples just send the invitation out three to four months before the wedding with an RSVP date of six to eight weeks ahead. This allows guests ample time to make any travel arrangements and ensures the bride and groom are not dealing with avoidable last-minute changes.

The number of guests will play a big part in deciding where to hold your wedding ceremony and reception. Before you can consider which venue is right for you, you will need to know how many guests you are inviting, your room layout, and what will physically be in each room (a dance floor, a stage, bars, buffet tables or food stations, tables, chairs, etc.). All of these event elements are determinants of room capacity, fire marshal approval, compliance with liquor licenses, and insurance requirements.

As you begin to review your guest list, focus only on the names, numbers, and table seating arrangement. Addresses and contact numbers, etc., will be filled out at a later date. Your main concern at this point is the number of guests attending, how many tables, and what size tables (e.g., tables of six, eight, ten, etc.) you will require. Remember to include in your count official guests such as your photographer, officiant, etc., if applicable. Again, work in pencil and make extra copies of worksheets if required. Always make sure to keep a blank master copy.

✧ Guest List Worksheet

Name(s):

_____

Address:

_____

_____

Contact Number(s):

_____

Gift Received:

_____

Special Notes/Meals:

_____

☐ Ceremony
☐ Reception
☐ Both
☐ RSVP Rec'd
☐ Gift Rec'd
☐ Thank You Card Sent

Of Guests _____
Table # _____

Name(s):

_____

Address:

_____

_____

Contact Number(s):

_____

Gift Received:

_____

Special Notes/Meals:

_____

☐ Ceremony
☐ Reception
☐ Both
☐ RSVP Rec'd
☐ Gift Rec'd
☐ Thank You Card Sent

Of Guests _____
Table # _____

Name(s):

_____

Address:

_____

_____

Contact Number(s):

_____

Gift Received:

_____

Special Notes/Meals:

_____

☐ Ceremony
☐ Reception
☐ Both
☐ RSVP Rec'd
☐ Gift Rec'd
☐ Thank You Card Sent

Of Guests _____
Table # _____

Name(s):

_____

Address:

_____

_____

Contact Number(s):

_____

Gift Received:

_____

Special Notes/Meals:

_____

☐ Ceremony

☐ Reception

☐ Both

☐ RSVP Rec'd

☐ Gift Rec'd

☐ Thank You Card Sent

Of Guests _____

Table # _____

Name(s):

_____

Address:

_____

_____

Contact Number(s):

_____

Gift Received:

_____

Special Notes/Meals:

_____

☐ Ceremony

☐ Reception

☐ Both

☐ RSVP Rec'd

☐ Gift Rec'd

☐ Thank You Card Sent

Of Guests _____

Table # _____

Name(s):

_____

Address:

_____

_____

Contact Number(s):

_____

Gift Received:

_____

Special Notes/Meals:

_____

☐ Ceremony

☐ Reception

☐ Both

☐ RSVP Rec'd

☐ Gift Rec'd

☐ Thank You Card Sent

Of Guests _____

Table # _____

Wedding Venue

Step 4 is all about selecting your perfect venue, but here are some considerations you should keep in mind as you create your vision. All wedding venues are not created equal. This is an important fact to keep in mind as you are making decisions on what matters most to you. Whether you choose a hotel ballroom, a wedding hall, a banquet room in a convention center, or a tent, your decision will affect the costs for tables, chairs, basic linens, china, crystal, and silverware, as all of these items are not necessarily included free of charge.

Your décor can be as simple as centerpieces or more elaborate, including custom chair covers, table coverings, specialty china and glassware, and some props. You can also have a full-out extravaganza with special effects, a stage show, and a complete audiovisual production. Take into account that rental costs often include charges for transporting the goods, labor for move-in, setup, on-site orchestration, teardown, and move-out. If anything is damaged or goes missing, you will be charged for its replacement.

The advantage to using an empty facility is that you can literally transform it into anything you want. With piping, draping, and special lighting effects, it can seem as though you are stepping into a different world. But dollars can run high; it all depends on what you choose to bring in.

Consider what you will have to do or bring into a room to give it the feel you are looking for. Look for venues that offer natural enhancements. For example, there is a hotel in California with a beautiful area overlooking the ocean that is perfect for an outdoor wedding. The hotel's linen, china, and glassware are exquisite and do not need upgrading. In inclement weather, the backup rooms have floor-to-ceiling windows and a covered terrace that still overlooks the ocean. Add a classical guitarist, lovely floral centerpieces, and candlelight and you have a beautiful setting. There is no additional cost for the ocean view, the garden setting, or the sunset.

Knowing what to look for is important. One private home that was available for daytime and evening weddings had lush gardens filled with gardenias and jasmine where a dance area could be set up. At night the gardenias and jasmine opened up and their heady fragrance perfumed the air. Timing, not cost, was the key to having an extra bonus or event enhancement.

The number of guests, the number of bar setups, food displays, type of décor, and entertainment all have to be factored into room capacity. You will need to clearly define your reception vision, so that you will be able to find the perfect room. Layout will also be an important factor, as you want to make sure that you do not create any areas of congestion by, for example, having all the bars in one location.

Having buffet tables and bars in the room will affect room capacity, as will a head table, décor, dance floor, stage, and any major audiovisual requirements. Other considerations are the number of guests that are to be seated at each table. Will you be having tables of six, eight, or ten, or a mixture? The venue will need to know what you envision taking place in your room. Layout will also impact room capacity.

Wedding Reception Styles

When planning your reception, there are a number of different options that you can look at and they can also affect your spending dollars.

Cocktail receptions generally last from one to two-and-a-half hours. If a dinner is to follow, the reception is usually one hour. If you are just having a cocktail reception, it can be extended up to two-and-a-half hours. What is important to keep in mind is what time the guests will be arriving and what time the wedding party and family members will be arriving (e.g., if they will be arriving late due to photographs being taken), as this will impact start and finish times. It is recommended to have scattered seating for your guests' comfort. Cocktail tables—short, tall, or a mix of both—to place empty glasses on for the waitstaff to collect should also be placed around the room. You need to give consideration to the length of your reception, your guests' age, and physical ability when calculating how many seats to provide.

With passed drinks and food, you can better control the amount being consumed and have service slowed down if things are moving too fast. You get the appearance of plenty without the expense; however, people tend to stay in one spot. They don't mix and mingle, and the energy of the room can grow stagnant. If drinks and food are coming to them, there is no incentive for the guests to circulate, so you'll want to set up icebreakers around the room to pull guests in. An icebreaker could be your guest book—people will gravitate to it to record their good wishes. Personal photo displays can also be set up around the room and a video of your courtship can be run continuously without sound, giving guests watching it something to say. Icebreakers can come in many forms, such as a specialty drink, musical entertainment, or an event element that ties into your wedding theme. You can also combine serving passed drinks and canapés with the addition of a couple of food tables set up with specialty items, such as a sushi bar; a pasta station; or a cheese, fruit, and crudité display. This will help to create movement and flow in the room.

If you decide to go with bar service instead of passed drinks, this will give guests another reason to walk about the room. As they stand in line, you have created another opportunity for guests to intermingle and meet.

Your service style will also play a part in creating room energy. A buffet dinner gets guests up and moving. If you are choosing to have a buffet, a two-sided buffet is recommended. It cuts down on congestion. A sit-down dinner is more formal and guests tend to remain seated until after the wedding speeches and toasts. If wine is served at the table, it is again a reason for guests to remain where they are and it adds a more polished presentation. If guests are required to go to the bar for beverages, you are strategically planning a way for them to meet other guests. It all depends on your wedding style, whether it is formal or informal, and what you want to achieve.

Cost Savings Considerations

As you begin to design your shared wedding vision, be on the lookout for ways to bring costs down or keep them in check. There are many ways that can be accomplished and they will not take away anything from your overall wedding vision. Examples of cost-saving considerations follow.

Location

- Look for a location that requires little in terms of décor enhancements and is a fit for the occasion. Some settings are perfect just as they are and don't require heavy décor to pull the look together.

Food & Beverage

- During receptions, people tend to take less food if it's passed by the waitstaff than if placed on a buffet table. The dual advantage is that you can order less food while guests still feel pampered.
- For buffet setups, consider smaller dessert-sized plates rather than luncheon or dinner plates. This generally results in people taking less food.
- If you want the feel of serving a high-end meal but need to save dollars, order half portions of two main entrée items. For example, combining a half portion of beef tenderloin with a half portion of chicken breast helps bring down the dollar cost per plate while still being able to offer guests a selection with depth.
- If you are planning a wedding reception and are flexible with the time of day, why not have a wedding brunch? Instead of serving your traditional evening

canapés, you could serve mini eggs benedict, bite size muffins, and little pastries. Accompany them with a selection of freshly squeezed juices, smoothies, tea, and coffee. This will definitely keep your alcohol price down as well as your food cost.

- Keep alcohol costs in check by serving one-ounce drinks instead of one-and-a-half ounces.

- Refrain from serving salty dry snacks, which encourage guests to drink more.

- One couple cut their champagne costs by having glasses of bubbly passed instead of poured or topped off. They did not want their guests to be able to put a dollar value on the quality of champagne that was being served and glasses were being replenished out of sight of the guests. Only select staff had access to top-of-the-line champagne and they refilled the VIP glasses from a very identifiable bottle. Guests attending the event left with the perception that they, too, were enjoying superior champagne.

- Escalating bar costs can be stopped by limiting the alcohol available, such as serving just wine and beer or creating a customized cocktail (alcoholic and nonalcoholic) and having it passed around during the reception.

- Have the wine stewards notify one of your attendants as to when you are approaching the halfway mark of your estimated liquor consumption. You can then make an informed decision on whether to slow wine/beverage service or close the bar earlier than scheduled.

- The cost for a professionally manned bar is less than setting up a self-serve bar where liquor can flow too freely and costs skyrocket.

- Know your guests. One couple spent unnecessary dollars setting up a mashed potato bar that sat untouched and left their high-fashion guests searching for low-carb options.

- Announcing last call only serves to drive up alcohol costs. Many guests tend to view last call as their last opportunity to stockpile drinks by ordering multiple rounds.

- Order sandwiches for entertainers and crew instead of serving the full banquet meal and have them set up in a separate room from your guests.

Décor

- Create a statement with one large decorative element rather than using fifteen décor elements around the room.

- Concentrate on a *wow* entrance treatment and look at table décor. Beautiful linens and centerpieces go a long way to creating a look or supporting a theme.

❧ See what the facility has on hand that you can use to further your look. Sometimes a hotel or venue will have colorful overlays, chair covers, and interesting centerpieces. Most of the time the facility will throw the incidentals in at no cost.

❧ Budget for the most bang. Tone on tone floral arrangements can have more visual impact and provide a feeling of lavish abundance than a more costly mixed floral grouping.

❧ When considering décor options, picture the room full. Do not spend excess money on décor items only the first few guests walking into the room will see, such as added décor or trimmings to the skirting on any of the tables. Think tabletop and up.

Entertainment

❧ If your guests do not dance, do not hire a more costly dance band. Instead, look at a good background trio to create an ambience. If they bring their own sound and lights, you can also save on technical costs.

Staging, Lighting, Audio, and Visual

❧ Gobos are an interesting and dramatic specialty lighting effect that is not expensive. A gobo is a silhouette pattern (could be both your names entwined) cut from metal or glass used to project images from a light fixture (spotlight) on any surface (could be the wall, dance floor, ceiling, or drape). You can use them in static lekos (remains stationary), which will be very inexpensive, or use them in intelligent lighting fixtures (moves around the room), which, of course, is more money.

❧ Lighting can add a feel of extravagance without the cost and can be changed throughout the night to transform the room dynamics.

❧ Creative lighting can add more than atmosphere to your event. Moving custom gobos were used at one wedding to light up the path to the main event. The cost was minimal, but the effect was showstopping.

❧ If you will be requiring staging for a dance band, specialty lighting, and audiovisual equipment, always make sure to get your technical director involved in venue choice before contracting. Room height, location of pillars, chandeliers, loading dock access, size of elevator, etc., can all effect costs. Your supplier can offer budget-saving solutions and creative options if they obtain staging knowledge of the room well in advance.

Management Fees

🌿 Ensure that you truly understand how much you are paying for wedding planning services. Some suppliers mark up their supplier invoices and accept cost-inflating commissions in addition to the original management fee that they quote. Be sure you know where your dollars are going.

Negotiation

🌿 When looking for budget-saving opportunities with suppliers, start first with the areas where the revenue will allow negotiations to go forward. If the supplier is already working with tight margins, it may be impossible for them to lower costs significantly.

🌿 One rule of successful negotiation is to always put your cards on the table and be prepared to walk away if necessary (e.g., if concessions are only on one side).

Wedding Suppliers

🌿 Seek out wedding suppliers who are open to negotiation and actively help you find creative ways to meet your budget objectives. Work with wedding suppliers who value your business.

🌿 Be up front with your wedding suppliers regarding budget limitations. Your suppliers need to know the budget in advance so they can adhere to it and look for ways they can bring costs down.

Taking all of this information into account, it is now time to combine your individual wedding visions and design a wedding ceremony and reception that embraces both of your dreams. Refer back to the Wedding Vision Questionnaire and now fill in your must-have choices and the compromises that work for both of you.

Our Wedding Date
- Our wedding date is: _____
- We are getting married in (location): _____
- Our preferred time to be married is at: _____

Bride's Family
- The immediate family members who will be part of our wedding ceremony are:

_____

Groom's Family
- The immediate family members who will be part of our wedding ceremony are:

_____

Wedding Party
- I/we will be walked down the aisle by: _____
- The number of people in our wedding party will be: _____
- Our ideal wedding party will/will not include: _____
    Maid/Matron of Honor: _____
    Bridal Attendants: _____
    Best Man: _____
    Groomsmen: _____
- We will/will not be having:
    Flower Girl: _____
    Ring Bearer: _____
    Ushers: _____
- The wedding party will/will not be invited to bring a guest: _____

Wedding Guests
- Our preference is for a small/large wedding: _____
- The ideal number we would like to limit our guest list to: _____
- Single guests will/will not be invited to bring a guest: _____
- The age range of the guests we will be inviting is: _____
- Children will/will not be invited to our wedding: _____
- There are/are not guests that may have special needs, such as handicap accessibility:

_____

- Guests who we would like to have at our wedding from out of town are: _____
_____

- Out-of-town guests will be making their own travel arrangements/staying with family:
_____

- We will/will not be getting together with our out-of-town guests for an organized func-
tion(s) such as: _____

Wedding Style:

- We have decided our wedding style will be: _____

Invitations

- Our preferred invitation style is: _____

Wedding Ceremony

- Our preference is for the wedding ceremony and the wedding reception to take place in (the
same location or two separate locations): _____
- We want our wedding ceremony to take place at (venue): _____
- We want our wedding reception to take place at (venue): _____
- We see the wedding ceremony taking place inside/outside: _____
- We see our wedding ceremony as being formal/informal: _____
- We see the wedding party wearing: _____
_____

- The wedding ceremony location in relationship to where we live is: _____
_____

- The wedding ceremony location in relationship to where our guests live is: _____
_____

- A bridal suite will/will not be required at the wedding ceremony location: _____

Wedding Ceremony Décor

- As the guests are arriving at the wedding ceremony, we envision they will be greeted by:
_____

- The wedding ceremony stage will be set: _____
- The flowers that we want at our wedding would be: _____
- We see them being tones of: _____
- Our wedding color scheme will be: _____

Wedding Ceremony Music

- As our wedding guests arrive, they will be listening to: _____
- The music for our bridal procession will be: _____
- The song that will signal the arrival of the bride will be: _____
- There will/will not be live musical performances as part of our wedding processional or ceremony: _____

Wedding Ceremony Lighting

- We see the wedding ceremony lighting as being: _____

Wedding Party Arrival

- The wedding party will arrive at the ceremony by: _____
- The bride will arrive by: _____
- The bride will be accompanied by: _____
- The groom will arrive by: _____
- The groom will be accompanied by: _____
- The bride will be coming from: _____
- The groom will be coming from: _____

Wedding Photographs at the Ceremony

- We will/will not be having professional wedding photographs, videos, or a live wedding webcast of our ceremony: _____

Wedding Vows

- What will be of utmost importance to us to have in our wedding ceremony is:

    _____

- The wedding ceremony will be conducted by: _____
- Our wedding vows will be traditional/vows tailored to us/written by us: _____
- The special family, cultural, or religious traditions that will be very meaningful for us to include are: _____
- We see the wedding processional unfolding: _____

    _____

- We see the wedding ceremony taking (length of time): _____
- After we are joined in matrimony and are exiting the wedding stage, what we see taking place is: _____

• The music that will be played as we are introduced to our guests and walk back down the aisle as husband and wife is: _____

Wedding Photographs Before or After the Ceremony

• We will/will not have family photographs taken before or after the ceremony and before our wedding reception: _____
• The backdrop we want to see in our wedding photographs: _____
• The wedding party will be transported to the photograph location and wedding reception by: _____

Wedding Reception Venue

• We will/will not have the wedding ceremony and wedding reception take place in the same location: _____
• If our reception is being held in a secondary location, it will/will not present any transportation concerns for our guests: _____
• We see our wedding reception taking place: _____
• The type of venue that would best suit our wedding reception: _____
• We see the wedding reception taking place inside/outside: _____
• We see our wedding reception as being formal/informal: _____

Wedding Reception Arrival

• We see our guests arriving at the venue in advance/after the arrival of the wedding party: _____
• We will/will not require something for the guests to do in the time between the ceremony and the wedding party arrival at the reception: _____
• We will/will not need a separate area in which to host the arrival and then move the guests into another room once the wedding party arrives: _____
• Seating will/will not be required for any or all of the guests: _____
• We will/will not be having a receiving line: _____
• We see our reception unfolding: _____
• We see our reception starting/finishing: _____

Wedding Reception Room Requirements

• We see the room being laid out: _____
• We see our reception being a stand-up reception with scattered seating/a sit-down affair with table seating for all guests: _____

- If we are including dinner, seating will be open/seating chart: _____
- There will/will not be food stations or buffet tables: _____
- Food will be passed/plated: _____
- Beverages will be served from bars set up in the room/beverages be served by waitstaff: _____
- The wedding party will be seated: _____
- The wedding cake will be positioned: _____
- A stage will/will not be required for speeches, the musicians, DJ, or entertainment: ____
- There will/will not be dancing: _____
- There will/will not be any audiovisual requirements—such as rear-screen projection, plasma screens, etc. that need to be factored into the room size requirements: _____

Wedding Reception Décor

- As the guests are arriving at the wedding reception, we envision that they will see: _____
- We see the décor being: _____
- We see the room having table settings/centerpieces/flowers: _____
- The colors we see in the room: _____
- How we see the room looking: _____

Wedding Reception Entertainment

- We will/will not be having a DJ, live musicians, a dance band, or piped in background music: _____
- The type of music that will be played: _____
- We will dance our first dance to: _____
- Our MC will be: _____

Wedding Reception Lighting

- We see the room being lit: _____

Wedding Reception Audiovisual

- We will/will not be having speeches: _____
- Podium or microphones will/will not be required: _____
- We will/will not have any audiovisual requirements: _____

Wedding Reception Food and Beverage

- The beverages we will be serving will include: _____
- Our bar will be a hosted bar/cash bar: _____
- We will/will not be providing champagne or any other beverage for toasting: _____
- The type of food we see being served at our wedding reception is: _____

Bridal Couple Departure

- There will/will not be any special fanfare as we depart: _____
- We will be spending our first night together (location): _____
- We will be transported from the wedding reception by: _____

Pre-Wedding Events

- We will/will not be having a bachelor/bachelorette party: _____

Wedding Rehearsal

- We will/will not be holding a wedding dress rehearsal: _____
- A rehearsal dinner will/will not be a part of our plans: _____
- We see it as being casual/formal: _____
- The ideal location in which to hold our rehearsal dinner is: _____
- Attending our rehearsal dinner will be just the wedding party/out-of-town guests will be open to attending as well: _____

Bride's Attire

- I will be buying, borrowing, or renting my wedding dress: _____
- If I will be wearing a wedding veil, I will be buying, borrowing, or renting it: _____
- If I will be wearing a headpiece, I will be buying, borrowing, or renting it: _____
- The jewelry I own that will I be wearing will be: _____
- The jewelry I will need to buy or borrow to complete my wedding look will be: _____
  _____
- I will be having my hair professionally done: _____
- I will be having my makeup professionally done/need to purchase: _____
- I will/will not be getting a professional manicure and pedicure: _____
- I will/will not need to buy special bridal shoes for the ceremony: _____
- Special lingerie I will need to buy: _____
- My something old will be: _____
- My something new will be: _____

- My something borrowed will be: _____
- My something blue will be: _____
- My wedding ring will/will not need to be purchased: _____
- I will/will not be wearing short, long, or any gloves: _____
- I will/will not need to purchase a small purse: _____
- I will/will not need to buy a garter: _____
- I will/will not be purchasing a special perfume for my wedding day: _____
- I will/will not be purchasing items to create a mini personal care pouch filled with essential wedding day aid items for the wedding party: _____
- I will/will not need a special going-away ensemble: _____
- I will/will not need to buy special going-away shoes: _____
- I will/will not need to buy going-away accessories: _____

Groom's Attire

- I will be wearing a formal tux, morning suit, or dress suit: _____
- I will be renting, buying, or wearing my own wedding clothing: _____
- I will be renting, buying, or wearing my own dress shoes: _____
- The personal clothing items I will need to buy: _____
- I will/will not need to purchase a wedding band: _____
- The grooming aids I will be requiring: _____
- I will/will not be having any professional grooming services done: _____
- The jewelry I own that I will I be wearing (e.g., cuff links, tie pin, watch, other): _____
- I will/will not need to purchase a special cologne: _____
- I will/will not need to buy going away apparel: _____
- I will/will not need to buy going away accessories: _____

Wedding Party Attire

- We will/will not be paying—in full or in part—for the wedding party attire: _____
- Being a part of wedding party—if we are not paying all expenses—will/will not be a financial hardship for anyone: _____
- We will/will not be giving gifts to all members of the wedding party: _____

Honeymoon

- We will/will not be going on a honeymoon immediately after the wedding, the next day, or at a later date: _____

- The perfect honeymoon destination for us is: _____
- We will be away (length of time): _____
- The amount we need to set aside for our honeymoon and expenses while we are away:

_____

Wedding Budget

- We will/will not be holding any pre-wedding events for out-of-town guests: _____
- We will/will not need to budget for bringing in special family members, wedding party, or guests to our wedding who may not be able to attend otherwise: _____
- We know—if our families are contributing to our wedding costs—the dollars they will be providing and the budget perimeters we need to be respectful of to ensure that there are no financial hardships incurred: _____
- If our families are helping us with wedding expenses, the money is being given as a gift for us to use towards our total costs/ there may be concessions that will need to be made:

_____

- In exchange for family financial assistance, we are/are not prepared to possibly compromise what may be important to us as a couple: _____
- Our personal spending budget is: _____
- What we are prepared to do to be fiscally responsible to ensure that we do not create financial hardships for ourselves or others (e.g., move date forward to give ourselves time to save, look for creative cost-saving options, carefully review our "must-haves" to weed out any wants, not needs): _____

_____

It's All under Control

Designing Your Realistic Blueprint

HAVING CREATED A shared wedding vision and determined your combined "must-haves," it is now time to revise your wedding flow overview and create a detailed blueprint of your wedding. Laying out your schedule of events and your wedding components step by step will also allow you to see the extent of your potential expenditures and where you may need to make adjustments, find creative areas of compromise, and look at cost-saving options. Your wedding day blueprint will also become the foundation for building your Critical Path (Step 7) and creating your Wedding Flow sheets (Step 8).

As you meet with your wedding vendors, you will begin to fill in the blanks with regard to spending, timing, and wedding logistics. A very clear path will begin to emerge—your wedding blueprint.

Creating Your Wedding Blueprint

ONE OF THE best methods for creating your Wedding Day Blueprint is to lay everything out on a spreadsheet that has been set up on your computer so that you can see easily how small changes can make a big difference in managing your budget. You will be able to play with different scenarios by adding and subtracting event elements to see where you have the best fit. You can also see what will happen to your budget in case you need to decrease or increase your guest count. For example, adding four more dinner guests does not necessarily mean just adding the cost of four more meals or beverages to your budget calculations. If your tables are already at maximum capacity, it could mean adding the cost of an extra table, chairs, table linens, table settings, centerpieces, wedding favors, etc. It is important to make sure that you set up costs as line items—menu style—so that you can clearly see what each inclusion costs and break out the applicable taxes, service charges, and miscellaneous fees so that there are no hidden costs. A blank Wedding Day Blueprint layout can be found at the end of this chapter.

You need to be able to compare costs "apples to apples" and you can't always do that by looking at the per person or lot cost. That does not give you the full story. Some suppliers show a low per person price or lot cost, but you need to make sure you're adding on all their true costs. These can be buried in the contract's fine print, in policies not clearly spelled out in the contract, or in language that is referring to pieces of information other than the contract itself. (For example, "any applicable costs outlined in our banquet menu," refers to material separate from the contract.) In the end, they could come in more expensive than a supplier who may have appeared to have a higher cost initially because they were disclosing their add-on fees up front. Having all costs spelled out allows you to choose the supplier who will best meet your needs and your price points, as well as helps you to walk away from a supplier who leaves you feeling wary of the way they are conducting business. The quote you receive from suppliers and how it is laid out can tell you volumes about their work ethics. You are looking to work with suppliers who have "transparency," where everything is up front, integral, open, and you can clearly see where your money is being spent.

Revised Wedding Flow Overview

Your Wedding Blueprint starts off with your proposed Wedding Flow overview, which will now be fine-tuned and based on your shared Wedding Vision. Walk through your day, systematically, visualizing each of your proposed wedding elements and identifying your main headings. Creating a new Wedding Flow overview takes you back to visualizing your wedding with the big picture in mind and you can start to build your wedding elements into your blueprint.

Your Wedding Day Blueprint allows you to see where you are and to be in a position to step back, look at the big picture, and take a moment to consider your creative cost saving options before rushing to contract. Food and beverage, entertainment, décor, and all of your other wedding elements are laid out in the same manner. Once everything has been brought to light, you can start to play with your options—adding and subtracting items—to see how they will affect your wedding vision must-haves and your wedding budget, and you can make decisions about optional wedding day enhancements.

Seeing costs for a buffet setup, for example, may move you to compare costs for a sit-down dinner, as having a buffet will necessitate having multiple plates, cutlery, etc. If you are holding your wedding in a hotel, this does not translate into additional charges, but if your wedding is being held at home or being catered at a private venue, this will be a cost consideration.

Inserting your proposed inclusions and estimated costs in the sequence they will occur will prompt you to see any problem areas. If the cost for flowers are all lumped together on your blueprint, it may be easy to miss the fact that the boutonnieres for the groomsmen have been overlooked. Visualizing what will be taking place under the wedding party heading and having them listed there lets you know they have been accounted for. It is a cross-check and cross-reference measure that professional event and wedding planners use to ensure that nothing has been overlooked. Items are left off contracts all the time and what will show up on your wedding day is only what was contracted. Setting out your blueprint in this manner works to bring you smoothly into your wedding day logistics and timing.

Using your new Wedding Vision and Wedding Flow sheets, begin to plot out your Wedding Day Blueprint. Right now you are creating your blueprint shell and as you begin to meet with your chosen suppliers, you will start to fill in the blanks with regard to inclusions and pricing. Keep your focus on your wedding day "must-haves." Optional enhancements can be listed and prices noted, but not included in your costs, once you begin to work through your blueprint.

As you are starting out, for quick calculations to see where you stand dollar-wise, budget backward. Take the total amount you are planning to spend on your wedding budget and divide it by the number of guests you plan to have. That will give you a per person cost. If, for example, your per person cost comes out at $60 and you are thinking about throwing a sit-down dinner, your guest list is out of line with your possible wedding inclusions. You will know that just from estimating the cost of dinner and drinks at a nice restaurant and comparing it to your per person figure, there would be no room for anything else in this scenario.

Going into debt is not the solution. You are designing a wedding day that is a celebration of your love, not one that will place you personally or those contributing to your wedding day at financial risk. If this is the situation you find yourselves heading toward, it is time to fine tune the timing of your wedding versus your savings ability, your guest list, your wedding style, or all three. An intimate sit-down dinner for fifty of your closest loved ones may be more genuine to who you are as a couple than a standup reception for three hundred that includes casual acquaintances and business associates. It can be looked upon as a gift—viewed in the proper spirit—to be guided back through your budget to staying true to who you are and your financial commitment. The process makes the decision making so much easier. To get a clear picture, once the shell of your wedding day blueprint is done, plug in rough estimates or your best guesses of costs and see how quickly the dollars add up. You'll be substituting real costs for those dollar amounts as you move forward, but in the meantime, building your budget backward will help you to get a handle on where you stand going in.

What to Include in Your Blueprint

Following is a list of the categories you will want to include in your Wedding Day Blueprint if you are creating your own spreadsheet. Remember to work in pencil and to keep a clean master copy. Always date your blueprint so that you know you are working with current information. Back up your blueprint on a disk and make sure that you have a hard copy printout of your final version.

- **Wedding Date and Number of Guests the Blueprint Is Based on**
- **Wedding Day Flow Overview**
- **Wedding Day Flow Blueprint Overview**
- **Advance Prep**

    Put supplier contractual critical paths and personal commitments in order by date (e.g., wedding party attire fitting, hair and makeup, rehearsal booking, etc.). Do not lay them out in total under their individual headings.

- **Move-In**

    Detail move-in requirements from suppliers for both wedding and reception in date and time order. This will give you a clear picture of the actual wedding flow, areas of overlap, and crunch time periods. Do not lay them out under separate headings.

- **Setup**

    Detail setup requirements from suppliers for both wedding and reception in date and time order. Do not lay them out under separate headings.

- **Rehearsal**
  List both supplier and personal rehearsal requirements in time order. Do not lay them out under separate headings.
- **Wedding Day**
  Detail both supplier and personal wedding day requirements in time order. Do not lay them out under separate headings.
- **Teardown**
  Detail teardown requirements from suppliers for both wedding and reception in date and time order. Do not lay them out under separate headings.
- **Move-Out**
  Detail move-out requirements from suppliers for both wedding and reception in date and time order. Do not lay them out under separate headings.
- **Post-Wedding**
  Detail post-wedding personal and supplier responsibilities in date and time order. Do not lay them out under separate headings.

Wedding Flow Blueprint Breakdown

This list gives you a variety of possible headings and subheadings to include in your Wedding Flow Blueprint. The more detailed your blueprint the better, so use this list as a starting point and add your own details to it.

Number of Guests

- Bride's Family
- Groom's Family
- Wedding Party
- Total Guest Count to Date

Wedding Style/Theme

Invitations

- Save the Date Cards (if applicable)
- Invitations
- Reply Cards
- Other print material (e.g., directional map)
- Related charges such as postage, calligraphy, etc.

Rehearsal

Rehearsal Dinner

Pre-Wedding Ceremony
- Personal Costs (hairstyling, manicure, etc.)
- Flowers for Wedding Party
- Photographs at Home
- Other related charges or expenditures, such as wedding party gifts, etc.

Wedding Ceremony

Transportation to the Wedding Venue

Wedding Venue Rental and Related Charges

Wedding Ceremony Décor

Wedding Ceremony Music

Wedding Ceremony Lighting

Wedding Ceremony Guest Arrival
- Any related charges such as valet parking, attendants with umbrellas to escort guests in inclement weather, snow removal, etc.

Wedding Party Arrival
- Any related charges

Wedding Photographs Before the Ceremony

Wedding Photographs at the Ceremony

Wedding Ceremony
- Related costs (e.g., payment to officiant, license, caretaker, etc.)

Wedding Photographs After the Ceremony
- Costs related to wedding photos

Wedding Party Transportation to Photographs and/or Wedding Reception

Wedding Reception Venue Rental Charges

Wedding Reception Guest Arrival
- Parking (valet or otherwise)
- Coat Check
- Attendants

Wedding Reception Wedding Party Arrival

Wedding Reception Décor

Wedding Reception Entertainment

Wedding Reception Lighting

Wedding Reception Audiovisual

Wedding Reception Photographs

Wedding Reception Food

Wedding Reception Beverage

Wedding Food and Beverage Rentals

Wedding Staffing

Wedding Cake Cutting Ceremony

Bridal Couple Departure

Wedding Party Departure

Guest and Supplier Communication Costs

- Estimated long distance charges
- Estimated courier costs
- Estimated fax charges
- Estimated photocopying charges

Additional Printing Charges

- Thank-you cards to suppliers
- Thank-you cards for wedding gifts
- Menus
- Other printed material

Permits and Special Licenses

Insurance

Security

Additional Staffing

Other Miscellaneous Wedding Day Charges

Personal Expenditures to Include in Budget

- Bride's Attire
- Groom's Attire
- Wedding Party Attire
- Honeymoon

Other Miscellaneous Personal Charges

Estimated Wedding Total

Once your Wedding Day Blueprint has been designed, you are ready to begin to research your venues and wedding suppliers. Having prioritized what is important to you, the process of elimination—should it become financially necessary—will be made easier and less emotional.

❧ Wedding Day Blueprint

Our Wedding Date: _____

Based On (# of guests): _____

Wedding Day Blueprint # _____ Date: _____

Our Wedding Theme _____

Wedding Timelines

	Quantity (if applicable)	Description	Cost	Deposit Paid	Balance of Payment
Advance Prep					
Move-in					
Setup					
Wedding					
Post-Wedding					
Teardown					

Proposed Wedding Flow

Invitations					
Save the Date Cards					
Invitations					
RSVP Cards					
Out-of-town Guest Air Transportation, Hotel, & Car Rental					
Out-of-town Guest Hotel					
Wedding Ceremony Site Rental Charges					
Wedding Ceremony Site Prep					

	Quantity (if applicable)	Description	Cost	Deposit Paid	Balance of Payment
Wedding Ceremony Site Décor, Lighting, etc.					
Permits					
Parking					
Photographer					
Guest Arrival					
Bridal Party Arrival					
Wedding Ceremony					
Bridal Party Departure					
Wedding Photo Shoot					
Wedding Reception Site Rental Charges					
Wedding Reception Site Prep					
Wedding Reception Site Décor, Lighting, etc.					
Permits					
Parking					
Photographer					
Guest Arrival					
Bridal Party Arrival					
Food					
Beverages					
Entertainment					
Power					
Trucking					

	Quantity (if applicable)	Description	Cost	Deposit Paid	Balance of Payment
Security					
Event Insurance					
Event Permits					
Communication Costs					
Wedding Team On-Site					

Estimated Wedding Ceremony & Reception Costs					

Personal Expenditures

Bridal Gown					
Bridal Accessories					
Hair and Makeup					
Going-Away Outfit					
Tuxedo					
Groom Accessories					
Groom Personal Grooming					
Wedding Party Costs					
Wedding Party Gifts					
Bridal Bouquets, Wedding Party Bouquets, etc.					
Wedding Rings					
Overnight Hotel					
Honeymoon					

Estimated Total Wedding Costs					

When It's Perfect, It's Easy

Choosing the Perfect Wedding and Reception Site

KNOWING WHAT IS right for you and what to look for makes finding the perfect wedding venue much easier. You will feel a strong emotional connection when the locale is exactly the right fit. You will know that you have found what you were looking for, and venues that will compromise your wedding vision will be ruled out as soon as you walk through the door.

Finding the Perfect Site for Your Wedding Ceremony and Reception

YOUR REQUIREMENTS FOR your wedding ceremony and your reception are very different, and it is better to look at them objectively as separate entities. While it may have been your original intention to have them in the same place or at separate locations, going in knowing your requirements allows you to take advantage of an unexpected possibility when it presents itself. Be flexible, but don't compromise.

Tentative Hold and Second Option

You can ask a venue to put space on "tentative hold." This allows you to reserve the space without a deposit or contract, so you'll have the time to make an informed decision. If another couple has already placed the venue on tentative hold, you can ask to be placed on "second option." The facility will then contact their other clients and give them a set date by when they must go to contract. If the other couple is not prepared to do so by their deadline, their tentative option will be dropped and the space will be offered to you. You must be prepared to sign the contract and make a deposit at this time, so make sure you have done your due diligence and uncovered all the costs that could apply. You can also ask to be placed on second option even if there is a deposit and contract in place. Should anything change (and it does happen), the venue will notify you that the date has opened up. By this time, you may have secured other space, so consider any applicable cancellation charges along with any other costs of making a move. It must make dollars and sense to do so. Don't be induced by high-pressure sales or scare tactics into contracting or moving unless it is truly in your best interests.

Determining Your Venue Requirements

In order to find the perfect venue, you have to look at your wedding ceremony and reception from a multitude of perspectives—yours, your wedding party's, your guests', and each of your wedding ceremony suppliers'. In actuality, "wedding suppliers" could be friends and family members who will be orchestrating some of these aspects on your wedding day, but think of them right now in terms of the service they will be providing. Many couples make the mistake of choosing a venue only considering one point of view. Their ceremony venue comes up short because key areas have been overlooked.

Consider poor planning consequences. For example, the bridal couple finds out after the fact that their guests couldn't hear or see their ceremony properly and their main recollection of their wedding was the entrance and exit. Another example is the wedding dress or veil got caught on the pew or chair decorations as the bride walked down the aisle and was required to stop constantly and untangle it. Imagine discovering that the couple's wedding ceremony photos were less than hoped for because the photographer's sightlines were blocked and they were unable to get a good vantage point from which to take pictures.

Use the Wedding Ceremony Requirements Questionnaire on the following pages to help you envision each venue from every point of view.

Advance Preparation

- Will we be required to take any courses (such as marriage courses) to be married in the facility or by the officiant? _____

- Does our facility have any dress restrictions that we must comply with, such as the bride and female attendants or our guests having covered arms or that heads must be covered? _____

- Does our wedding site venue have any restrictions as to the type of music that is played or what décor that is brought in? _____

Our Wedding Rehearsal

- Will we be requiring access to the wedding ceremony site for a rehearsal? _____

Ushers' Arrival

- Will our ushers require early access to storage rooms to obtain any items for guest arrival? _____

- How early will we require someone be there to open the doors and assist them? _____

- Does our facility provide services to vacuum the entrance and wedding ceremony site in case décor items or people moving equipment in have left a mess? Is this something that we will have to make special arrangements for or will our ushers need to attend to this? _____ _____

Ushers' Responsibilities and Weather Considerations

- Does our venue supply oversize umbrellas for our ushers to use to help escort guests should there be inclement weather or would we need to provide them? _____

- What other weather considerations, based on the timing and season of our wedding, do we need to check with our venue to see how they are handled so that we can advise our ushers of their procedures? _____

- Will any weather considerations need to be factored into our budget? _____

- For summer, late spring, and early autumn weddings, is there air-conditioning available if needed and is it provided free of charge or at an additional cost? _____

- For winter, early spring, and late autumn weddings, what does our facility have in place for snow removal; de-icing of parking, walkways, and stairs; sweeping of leaves from the walkways; coat check or rack; umbrella and boot check? Is this supplied and staffed at no cost or will this be an additional requirement we need to book and expense in advance?_____

Family and Guest Arrival

- Will there be adequate parking for all our guests? _____

- Do we require a site that can be reached by public transportation? _____

- How far will our guests have to walk from public transportation or parking to reach our venue? _____

- Will we need reserved parking for specific family members—parking that has easy access for arrival and an unobstructed departure for the wedding shoot? _____

- Will we need a venue that can accommodate valet parking? _____

- Will we need to look at bringing in a directional traffic officer? _____

- What venue amenities will we need to look for in regards to our family's and guests' arrival and comfort? For example, if our wedding is taking place in the heat of summer do we need to take into account air-conditioning—and if it is required to be running—how will our extra electrical requirements affect the facility's electrical output? _____

_____

- If we are holding the wedding ceremony outside and not tenting the area, are there shade areas for our guests? _____

- If no air-conditioning or shade is available, do we need to consider adding custom hand fans as a comfort touch to our wedding elements? _____

- Does the facility provide a bad weather backup room that will be reserved for us should the weather not permit us to hold our wedding ceremony outside? _____

- Are restrooms readily available and easily accessible for our guests? _____

- Will the restrooms be open, cleaned, maintained, and serviced during the time we are there? _____

- Are there sufficient restrooms on hand to handle our guest size or will we be required to bring additional facilities in as per fire marshal and health regulations? _____

- Is the venue handicapped equipped? _____

- Will we require cleared closet space or hanging racks and hangers for guests' outerwear to be hung? Are these provided or do we need to have these brought in? _____

- Will we require coat check staff to be on hand? Is this an additional cost to us if we want to have the coat check manned? _____

- What room capacity would we need to plan for to ensure maximum comfort for our guests?

_____

- Are there any areas of congestion or bottlenecks that could take place? _____

_____

Wedding Suppliers during the Ceremony

• If any of our wedding suppliers are on hand during the ceremony, do we require a separate holding room for them or will they be sitting with our guests during the ceremony?

_____

Music during the Ceremony

• What are the room acoustics like? _____

• If any other event is taking place in the same venue, how soundproof is the room?

_____

Wedding Photos during the Ceremony

• What type of pictures do we want taken at arrival, during the ceremony, and when we depart? _____

• How are the room's sightlines? Are there any pillars that will block our guests' view? Are there hanging chandeliers that will mar our wedding photographs? _____

_____

• Will we require an overhead vantage point for photographers or video operators to take pictures from a different angle? _____

• Based on the room layout, how many photographers will we need to have on hand to cover the different shots and be able to easily move from area to area? _____

• What type of lighting will we require for the photographs? _____

Groomsmen's Arrival

• Will we need reserved parking for our groomsmen that has easy access for arrival and an unobstructed departure for the wedding shoot? _____

• Will we need an area for our groomsmen to gather and to be able to safely store their personal effects? _____

Groomsmen's Responsibilities

• Will our groomsmen be playing a part in any family, cultural, or personal touches or traditions that require any special considerations or authorization from the venue? _____

_____

Best Man's Arrival

• Will we need reserved parking for the best man that has easy access for arrival and an unobstructed departure for the wedding shoot? _____

• Will we need a separate room for our best man to use and to be able to safely store his personal effects or will he be using the same room as our groomsmen? _____

Best Man's Responsibilities

• Will our best man be playing a part in any family, cultural, or personal touches or traditions that require any special considerations or authorization from the venue? _____

_____

Wedding Official's Arrival

• Will we need reserved parking for the wedding official? _____

• Will we need a secure room for our wedding official to use and to be able to safely store his or her personal effects separate from the groomsmen and best man? _____

• Will our wedding official require anything special brought in, such as a table, chairs, or a private area for the signing of the marriage license? _____

_____

Wedding Official's Responsibilities

• Will our wedding official be playing a part in any family, cultural, or personal touches or traditions that require any special considerations or authorization from the venue? _____

_____

Groom's Arrival

• Will we need reserved parking for the car transporting the groom? _____

• Will we need a separate room for the groom to finishing dressing, relax out of sight of our wedding guests, or to be able to safely store his personal effects? _____

Bridal Attendants' Arrival at the Church

• Will we need reserved parking for the bridal attendants that has easy access for arrival and an unobstructed departure for the wedding shoot? _____

• Will we need a secure room for them to use and to be able to safely store their personal effects? _____

• Will we require access for our bridesmaids to a separate bathroom, away from the guests, for last-minute touch-ups? _____

Bride's Arrival at the Church

• Will we need reserved parking for the car transporting the bride that has easy access for arrival and an unobstructed departure for the wedding shoot? _____

• Will we require access to a private room or bathroom, away from the guests, to finish dressing or for last-minute touch-ups? _____

Wedding Processional

• How wide will the aisle need to be for the wedding party processional we envision? What does the number of people side by side, style of dress, and pew décor need to be to allow us to move effortlessly down it and not brush against the guests or get caught on chair ends? _____

• Does the wedding look we are envisioning require the bride, maid or matron of honor, or bridesmaids to be in high heels? Do we need to keep an eye out for difficult staircases to go down and up with grace due to the height of our shoes or length of our dresses? Is there any open grating in the floor that could cause someone to catch their heel, or dress, and stumble or trip? _____

Wedding Ceremony

• How long do we envision our wedding ceremony service being? _____

• Will our wedding ceremony include any family, cultural, or personal touches or traditions that require any special considerations or authorization from the venue?_____

_____

Bride and Groom Introduction to Guests

• Will our introduction to our guests as a married couple include any family, cultural, or personal touches or traditions that require any special considerations or authorization from the venue? _____

Wedding Photographs Before or After the Ceremony

• Will we want wedding photographs to be taken before the ceremony? _____

• Will we want wedding photographs to be taken at our wedding ceremony location after the ceremony? _____

• Will this be the setting for the majority of our wedding pictures taken after the ceremony, will we be moving to another location, or will we be going directly to the wedding reception?

_____

Our Departure from the Wedding Ceremony Site

• Will our departure have family, cultural, or personal touches or traditions that require any special considerations or authorization from the venue, such as a dove or butterfly release? _____

Wedding Party Departure

• Will all of our wedding party attendants have access to transportation to our wedding photograph location or do we need to make special arrangements? _____

Family and Guest Departures

• Will family members who will be part of our formal wedding pictures have access to transportation to our wedding photograph location or do we need to make special arrangements? _____

• Due to the number of guests we have coming, do we need to look at adding a directional traffic officer at the wedding ceremony departure to ease the situation of everyone leaving at one time? _____

• Do we need to look at traffic flow? _____

• Will any family or friends need to remain behind to gather any décor items? _____

• Will they need any assistance tearing down or transporting our décor items? _____

• How much time will they require and will it delay their arrival at our reception? _____

• How much time will our guests need to travel from our wedding ceremony site to our wedding reception? _____

Wedding Suppliers' Move-in Requirements

• Could our wedding suppliers' move-in be scheduled on the heels of another event or wedding's move-out? Will this cause any problems to our move-in or cause us to have additional expenses? _____

• Do we know what responsibility the venue will bear if their other client's teardown and move-out causes ours to be delayed? _____

• What type of parking (e.g., large trucks, small trucks, or cars) could our wedding suppliers require? _____

• What kind of delivery access to the site could our suppliers need? _____
_____

• Will we be having a multitude of suppliers making deliveries over the course of several days, all day long on one specific day, or just one main delivery? _____

- Will our wedding suppliers be required—based on our wedding vision at this point, not on actual wedding supplier requirements—to bring in any large, heavy, or awkward to carry items?
_____

- Could our suppliers require special equipment being brought in at an additional cost to unload and move in these items? _____

- Is a venue that has a ramp or loading dock preferable? _____

- Will our wedding suppliers' move-in crews encounter any difficulties with what we are proposing? _____

- Will they be able to maneuver through the doors, make their way through the aisles, and up, down, and around staircases? _____

- What will we need to keep an eye out for that could facilitate an easy move-in (e.g., service elevators)? _____

- What type of items and in what kinds of quantity will we be having delivered to the wedding site? _____

- Will the site layout and timing of the move-in require our wedding suppliers to bring in extra staff, at additional cost, to facilitate a faster move-in? _____

Wedding Suppliers Setup Logistics

- Which of our wedding suppliers will require move-in and setup access to our ceremony site the week prior, several days ahead, or the day before our wedding? _____

- Will we need to put a twenty-four-hour hold on any of the spaces we are reserving? _____
_____

- Do we know exactly how much time the wedding suppliers who are moving in and setting up on the actual day of our wedding will require? _____

- Have we taken into account how the timing of each suppliers' move-in and setup could impact our other suppliers? _____

- Do we know the sequential order in which our suppliers need our move-in and setup to occur? _____

- Is there anything else taking place at the venue or otherwise that could cause our wedding suppliers to be delayed (e.g., construction, renovations, or labor contract disputes)?
_____

- Will our wedding suppliers be focused on our wedding move-in and setup or juggling multiple set ups and events on the same day that could result in timing difficulties for us? How tightly do they book their services? _____

- What prep work will we be required to do in advance of our supplier move-in? For example, tent installations may require that cable lines, gas lines, hydro lines, and water lines may need to be identified and marked before installation can begin. In addition, it may require lawn grooming, vacuuming, insect prevention, tree branches tied back or raised, and sprinkler systems turned off. _____

_____

- Will any of our wedding suppliers require a locked storage area? If so, how large would it need to be to hold our proposed items (e.g., wedding canopy, pillars, or any other major décor prop, or large quantities of small items, such as containers of bubbles or individual packets of rose petals)? _____

_____

- How long could our suppliers conceivably require the storage space? Will they need it from move-in, setup, during our reception and possibly afterwards, or until teardown and move-out can take place? _____

- Will any of our wedding suppliers have any special requirements that we need to be aware of and make sure are available to them (such as access to running water or refrigeration)?

_____

- Do we know what electrical power, if any, each of our wedding suppliers possibly requires?

_____

- Have we taken stock of electrical outlets and mapped out where they are located in relation to supplier requirements and room layout? _____

- Will our proposed layout result in visible wires showing that will need to be covered or secured (taped so that guests do not trip) or require that extension cords be brought in?

_____

- Have we alerted the venue as to how much total power will be used by all of our suppliers and whether the facility can safely accommodate this? _____

- Do we need to bring in an electrical technician to confirm that the suppliers' needs can be safely met or advise us whether or not we need to consider a backup generator to ensure there are no power black-outs? _____

- Does the venue have on-site security to ensure there is no theft or damage to wedding supplier goods between move-in, setup, and our wedding ceremony or will we be required to provide it? _____

- Does the facility have any noise restrictions that we need to make our suppliers aware of, such as noise related to building of any custom items, how loud the music can be played, and if there are noise curfews? _____

- Based on the type of décor we want to bring in, will we need to check the facility's rules regarding use of tacks or any other fastenings for walls, chairs, tables, etc., so that we can advise our suppliers? _____

- To make sure that our wedding suppliers are aware of and will adhere to our wedding venue's policies, do we need to add an addendum to their contracts so that we don't incur any charges for damage? _____

- Do we know what type of insurance and for what coverage amount will be required by the venue from us and our wedding suppliers? _____

- Do we know if there are any special permits or licenses we or our suppliers will be required to obtain (e.g., fire marshal permit for any special effects, liquor license, building permit)? _____

- Do we know the venue and fire marshal rulings and regulations regarding items such as having candlelight or votives with open flames? _____

- Will open flames be permitted or will we need to look at an alternative such as Candle Safe (www.candlesafe.ws)? _____

- If the venue only has one parking lot and space is limited, do we need to look at alternate parking spots for them so that our guests are not inconvenienced? _____

- Could anything else be going on at our wedding ceremony site at the same time as our move in and set up that could inconvenience or delay our wedding suppliers? _____ _____

- Does the type of venue we are looking at lend itself to multiple wedding ceremonies? _____

- Could this impact the timing and logistics for move-in and setup of our wedding suppliers, inconvenience our guests, or interrupt our wedding ceremony in any manner (e.g., noise if they are setting up for another wedding during our ceremony)? _____

- Will our wedding suppliers need early access to the wedding ceremony site on the day of the wedding? _____

- Can the facility accommodate early access and are there any additional charges we need to be aware of to do this? _____

- Will our wedding suppliers still be on-site when the guests arrive and is there a separate parking area for them? _____

Wedding Suppliers' Teardown

- Will any suppliers be tearing down and moving out décor after our wedding ceremony has concluded and guests have departed? _____

- How much time will they require? _____

- Could our wedding suppliers' teardown and move-out be extensive? _____

- Will we require extra time from the venue to allow them to move out the same day? _____

• Could our wedding suppliers conceivably require storage space after the wedding?

_____

• Will there be another event or wedding party moving in as our wedding suppliers are moving out? How much time do they have to tear down the wedding ceremony site and move out? _____

• How does that impact our wedding suppliers with regards to timing and logistics? Will they be required to bring in extra staff in order to tear down and move out quickly to accommodate the other couple's move-in and setup? _____

• Do we need to extend the time we have blocked to accommodate our wedding suppliers' teardown and move-out? _____

• Are there any possible overtime charges that could apply that we need to budget for?

_____

Family and Guest Arrival

• Will there be adequate parking for all our guests? Are there parking restrictions we need to be aware of or any parking permits that need to be obtained? _____

• Will we need reserved parking for specific family members that has easy access for arrival after the wedding photo shoot as they will be arriving after the guests? _____

• Will we need a venue that can accommodate valet parking? _____

• Will we need to look at bringing in a directional traffic officer? _____

• Will we require a site that can be reached by public transportation? _____

• How accessible is the transportation from our wedding ceremony site to our wedding reception site? How often does it run on that specific day of the week? How late does it run? Could any of our guests be left stranded without a way home? _____

_____

• How far would guests have to walk from public transportation or parking to reach our venue? _____

• Will our guests be proceeding directly to the wedding reception or will there be a lapse of time while we have our wedding photographs taken? _____

• What do we have planned for our guests while we take our wedding photographs? Do we require a separate room in which refreshments can be served before we open the doors on our arrival to the main reception and dining area? _____

• What venue amenities will we need to look for in regards to our family and guests' arrival and comfort? _____

• How will our total extra electrical requirements affect the facilities electrical output?

_____

- If we are holding the wedding reception outside and not tenting the area, are there shade areas for our guests? _____
- Does the facility provide a reserved backup room in case of bad weather? _____
- Are restrooms available and easily accessible? Are they cleaned, maintained, and serviced during our event? _____
- Are there sufficient restroom facilities on hand to meet fire marshal and health regulations for the number of guests we have attending or will we be required to bring additional restrooms in (e.g., portable restrooms)? _____
- Is the venue handicapped equipped? _____
- Will we require space for guests' outerwear to be hung? Do we need to bring in coat racks, hangers, and coat check staff? _____
- What room capacity will we need to plan for taking into account receiving lines, tables for seating, head table, and whatever else may be in the room such as décor, bar setups, food stations, a dance floor, stage, etc.? _____
- Are there any areas of congestion or bottlenecks that could take place? Is there a clear path from the kitchen and service area to our guests? Can a receiving line be accommodated with our proposed room layout? _____
- Will our wedding ceremony have family, cultural, or personal touches or traditions that require any special considerations or authorization from the venue? _____
- How long do we envision our wedding reception taking place? What are our anticipated start and finish times? Do we need to make provisions for extended hours or an extended liquor license? _____

Wedding Suppliers during the Reception
- If any wedding suppliers are on hand during the ceremony, do we require a separate holding room for them or will they be sitting with our guests during the reception and invited to partake in food and drink? _____

Music during the Reception
- What are the room acoustics like? _____
- If any other event is taking place in the same venue at the same time, how soundproof is the room? _____

Wedding Photos during the Reception
- What type of pictures do we want taken at our arrival at the reception, during the reception, and when we depart? _____

- What do the room sightlines need to be like? _____

- Will we require an overhead vantage point for photographers or video operators to take pictures from a different angle? _____

- How many photographers will we need to have on hand to cover the different shots and be able to easily move from area to area? _____

- What type of lighting will we require for the photographs? What equipment will be brought in? _____

Wedding Party's Arrival at the Wedding Reception

- Will we need reserved parking for the wedding party that has easy access for arrival after the wedding shoot? _____

- Is there a separate entrance for the wedding party to use upon arrival? _____

- Will we need an area for our wedding party to gather and to be able to safely store their personal effects? _____

Our Arrival at Our Wedding Reception

- Will we need reserved parking for us that has easy access for arrival and an unobstructed departure for us to leave the reception before the guests? _____

- Will we require access to a private room or bathroom, away from the guests, for last-minute touch-ups before we make our entrance to our wedding reception or to change into our going away outfits? _____

Receiving Line

- How long and wide will the aisle need to be for our receiving line need to be? _____

Bride and Groom Introduction to Guests

- Will our introduction to our guests include any family, cultural, or personal touches or traditions that might require any special considerations or authorization from the venue?

_____

Wedding Reception

- How do we see our wedding reception unfolding? _____

_____

- Will our wedding reception include any family, cultural, or personal touches or traditions that might require any special considerations or authorization from the venue? _____

_____

• Will there be wedding toasts and speeches? When will these take place? _____

_____

• Will we have a cake cutting ceremony? _____

Wedding Photos during the Reception

• Will we have wedding photos taken during the reception from arrival until our departure?

_____

Our Departure from the Wedding Reception Site

• Will we be having a traditional garter or bouquet throwing and fanfare at our departure?

_____

• Will our departure have family, cultural, or personal touches or traditions that require any special considerations or authorization from the venue? _____

Family, Guest, and Wedding Party Departure

• Because of the number of guests we have coming, do we need to look at adding a directional traffic officer at the wedding ceremony departure to ease the situation of everyone leaving at one time? _____

• Do we need to look at traffic flow? _____

• Will any family or friends need to remain behind to gather any décor items? How much time would they require? _____

Wedding Supplier Teardown and Move-Out

• Will the caterer, décor, music and entertainment, and other wedding suppliers' teardown be extensive? _____

• Will we require extra time from the venue to allow them to move out the same day? _____

• Will they conceivably require storage space? _____

• Will special equipment or extra staff be required to expedite move-out? _____

• Will there be any overtime charges that could apply? _____

• Is cleanup included in the cost of the site rental and wedding supplier charges? _____

• What extra charges could we expect at final billing (e.g., power charges)? _____

• Will there be another event or wedding party moving in as our wedding suppliers are moving out? _____

• When do we have to be out of the room? _____

Begin to Gather Information

Professional wedding and event planners know to start their research over the telephone, starting with an introductory telephone call. They then fax or email all of their requirements over, as well as a wedding ceremony overview, and request that the venue get back to them with available options, prices, and a full sales kit including floor layouts, food and beverage menus (if applicable), terms, conditions, general rental agreement policies, etc.

By putting everything in writing, you'll spend less time on the telephone and have written backup as to what was requested and quoted. You'll eliminate countless hours of viewing unsuitable sites. It doesn't matter if the venue you are considering is down the street or halfway around the world, you must find out if there is availability on your dates, if the venue can meet your space requirements, and, if not exactly, whether it has a viable solution that could possibly work. For example, one hotel in New Orleans did not have space at the hotel to accommodate the wedding ceremony and reception over the requested dates. However, it did have exclusive access to a private home with a gorgeous courtyard where the wedding ceremony and reception could be held and that the hotel would cater. The hotel also supplied the tables, chairs, linens, dinner service, and glassware from the hotel and there would be no additional rental charges for these items.

You want to make sure that you limit your viewing—be it for your wedding ceremony or wedding reception—to sites that can meet your wedding must-haves and space requirements. Do not clutter your mind or waste your time doing site inspections before you have thoroughly researched your options and know that the venue is a possible consideration. Room rental fees and any other applicable charges don't come into play until you find out whether there is a fit or a specific reason to proceed further.

For a list of possible wedding ceremony sites, begin by checking with your local tourist board or the Internet. With destination weddings growing, a number of tourist boards have pamphlets that specifically feature wedding ceremony sites and reception options. You can also begin by attending local bridal shows. While bridal salons, florists, caterers, and wedding photographers are other sources, you can easily be pulled off track from your mission of doing what you need to do when it matters most and get caught up discussing other areas. You may not know at this stage whether or not what they are selling will be a match for your wedding ceremony site, or if the venue they are recommending is right for you or right for *them*—they may be the preferred supplier or be receiving a referral fee. Family, friends, and close work associates who have a vested interest in your happiness and who know your style can be excellent resources as well. But use caution when soliciting advice, listening to the swirl of what others would do can cause wedding information overload, chaos, confusion, and even hurt feelings if someone feels their suggestion was dismissed. You are also opening the door to expectation, as in the expectation of receiving a wedding invitation, and you need to tread carefully here. If you are asking advice from someone you do not intend to invite to your wedding celebration, it could cause a rift between you. There is a wealth of information available out there through a variety of sources. What is important is to keep your focus on your wedding vision and not get caught up in someone else's. If your request for space and the venue's availability are a match, you then move into finding out how much the facility will cost to rent. Use the Questionnaire for Each Venue, making enough copies to complete one for each proposed ceremony and reception venue.

What Your Proposed Venue Will Need to Know

INITIAL FACTS YOUR proposed wedding ceremony and reception venues will need to know include:

- The date the reception will take place
- The time the reception will take place
- How long the reception will be
- What time you will need access to the room
- What time you will be departing the room
- How many guests will be in attendance
- Anything else you will be bringing into the room (e.g., décor, music, entertainment, audiovisual, etc.)
- How you want the room laid out
- Whether you require any additional space to be held (e.g., additional rooms, storage, etc.) and, if so, what type of space, room capacity, and time duration you need
- Whether you will have any food and beverage requirements or whether you are just looking at renting the site
- Whether you will be holding a rehearsal and, if so, what date and time
- Any other special requirements you may have

- What are all the room rental charges (setup, rehearsal, wedding day, move-out, etc.) that could apply? _____

_____

- What are all the taxes that could apply? _____

_____

- What are all the service charges that could apply? _____

- How are the taxes and the service charges calculated? Are they charged only on the room rental rate or is the service charge taxed as well? _____

_____

- Are there any costs involved for staff? _____

- What other services could we conceivably be charged for (e.g., parking attendants, coat check staff, site security, etc.)? _____

_____

- What color and material are the walls? _____

- What color, pattern, and material is the flooring? _____

- How high are the ceilings? _____

- How are the sightlines? _____

- How are the acoustics in the room? _____

- What type of in-house sound, lighting, audiovisual, piped-in music systems, etc., do you have? _____

- Are there additional charges to use your system? _____

- What type of seating do you provide and are there any charges associated with this (e.g., chair rental, labor for setup, etc.)? _____

_____

- What other charges could be billed at final reconciliation (e.g., power charges, room cleaning, recovery charges—staff and cherry pickers for retrieving escaped helium balloons from the ceiling, etc.)? _____

_____

- What is the legal room capacity of the specific rooms we are considering? _____

- For outside events, is there a backup room in case of bad weather that will be on hold for us?

_____

- If we have to move our ceremony inside, will there be any additional costs we need to be aware of? _____

- What is the parking capacity? _____

- Is your venue handicap accessible? _____

- Could anyone else be holding an event in your facility at the same time? _____

- Will we be required or are you required to obtain any special permits? _____
_____

- What insurance coverage do you have? Will our suppliers or will we be required to obtain special occasion insurance? _____

- What fire marshal requirements will we need to comply with (e.g., can we have candles, etc.)? _____

- What are your policies with regard to fastening items to the walls, tables, chairs, etc.?
_____

- Is your venue unionized? How could this affect our labor costs? When are labor negotiations next taking place (are there possible concerns for a strike)? _____
_____

- When were renovations last done? _____

- When are renovations or construction next scheduled to take place? _____

- Have you held weddings at your facility before? _____

- Do you have letters of reference or people we can call? _____
_____

- Do you have a preferred supplier list that we must use or are we free to bring in our own wedding suppliers? _____

- How is access in and out of your facility for supplier move in and move out? _____
_____

- Can you send us your quote in writing, a full sales kit, room layouts, a sample contract, cancellation and payment schedule, and place the space on tentative hold? _____
_____

What to Inspect During Your Site Inspection

Keep to your agenda during the site inspection. If the venue does weddings on a regular basis, they may have seen something that may be perfect for you once they know your wedding vision. What you need to see is what is important to you, your guests, your suppliers, and your wedding design. Your suppliers will need to know what to expect. They will be calling the facility as well and may even do a site inspection of their own once you have narrowed your choice of venue down, before doing a walk-through with you during a formal site visit. You need to be familiar with what your wedding suppliers are telling you and able to visualize the areas that they are talking about.

It is extremely important when viewing the sites for your reception that you pay close attention to the facilities that their food and beverage staff or your caterer will be requiring on top of your other supplier needs. Keep an eye out for cleanliness in all areas; make a point of visiting both the male and female restrooms; and spot check the dishes, glassware, and the cutlery (if they are supplying). While spot checking the glasses at one of their proposed sites, one couple found dried pulp on the inside of a number of glasses. Another couple discovered table settings with chips and cracks. Table linens should also be examined for burns, tears, stains, and visible mending.

During the site inspection, you may be asked about contracting. Knowing the cost of the wedding ceremony venue is only half of the equation. You need to assess total costs, wedding ceremony costs, and reception costs to make an informed decision. If the site has great appeal, ask to have it placed on tentative hold so that you can have time to bring together all your costs and supplier requirements.

How to Narrow Your Choices

Narrow your choices by doing a cost comparison of the options that best fit your space, supplier, and guest needs, and your wedding vision. Lay all costs out on your Wedding Day Blueprint and see how the costs tally up. Compare the costs to the benefits in each of your final choices. One or two should stand out noticeably from the others, but before signing any contracts for your wedding ceremony, you need to know where you stand in total expenditures. At this moment, you only have part of the equation. Once you know all other costs, you will be in a stronger position to negotiate with your wedding venues and suppliers. You will know where you have to cut costs, by exactly how much, and be able to say specifically to your vendors that this is what we need to happen in order for us to move forward to contract. You will be negotiating for a property you want to do business with, not spending time going back and forth with a venue that is not right for you. Your energy is spent on finding areas of creative compromise and solutions that are equally beneficial to both sides. Your supplier is likely to work harder to find areas of negotiation when they know you are really interested in what they have to sell and are not merely shopping around.

What You Will Require from the Venue before You Can Finalize—Not Sign—Your Site Contract(s)

You will want to assemble all of the following information for each venue that you're considering.

- Written quote laid out in menu format, with all applicable taxes, service charges (and how they are calculated), and any other charges that will be billed at final reconciliation
- Sample contract for your review
- Sample payment schedule for your review
- Attrition dates (dates you can reduce guest numbers without penalty)
- Number guarantee dates (dates you must guarantee the number of guests)
- Cancellation charges
- Venue terms and conditions
- Venue policies
- Full sales kits complete with room layouts, capacity, and terms and conditions for each one of your applicable wedding suppliers and vendors, such as decorator, florist, food and beverage, entertainment, audiovisual, staging, and lighting
- Color numbers for wall and floor coverings (ask for Pantone numbers, as these are universal color numbers)

Venue Research Tips

- Keep in mind the number of guests you are planning to invite.
- Remember that tables, chairs, bar setups, buffets, food stations, a dance floor, etc., all take away from floor space.
- Consider whether you will need to remove items to create extra space. Find out if there is a storage area. Moving trucks can be used to store excess furniture—make sure the contents are insured against theft and damage.
- Always check to see if there is a clear path to and from the kitchen.
- Confirm whether there are any noise restrictions in your area.

🌿 Find out if the bathrooms and septic tanks will be able to handle the number of invited guests or if you will need to bring in backups such as portable bathroom trailers.

🌿 Always find out the legal room capacity, if there are any fire marshal rulings to be aware of, or required permits or host and supplier liability insurance that you will be required to obtain from each and every wedding supplier.

🌿 Know what is going on before your wedding, after your wedding, and during your wedding with regards to move-in, setup, actual events, teardown, and move-out, and how it could affect your wedding (e.g., noise, block access for move in, etc.).

🌿 Find out from your wedding ceremony and reception venues if they are handling only your event that day or holding back-to-back events in your room.

🌿 Find out how nonsmoking laws will affect you and what are the consequences.

🌿 **Cocktail Reception**

Allow eight square feet per person. Plan seating to accommodate a maximum of one third of the guests in addition to seating for elderly/handicapped guests.

🌿 **Cocktails with Food Stations**

Allow twelve to fifteen square feet per person.

🌿 **Seated Dinner**

Allow twenty square feet per person.

🌿 **Buffet Setups**

Request double-sided buffet stations for better guest service.

🌿 **Dinner Tables**

- A 72-inch table seats ten to twelve guests (132-inch floor length tablecloth rounds).
- A 60-inch table seats eight to ten guests (120-inch floor length tablecloth rounds).
- A 54-inch table seats six to eight guests (114-inch floor length tablecloth rounds).
- A 48-inch table seats four to six guests (108-inch floor length tablecloth rounds).
- A 36-inch table seats four guests (96-inch floor length tablecloth rounds).

🌿 **Bars**

Request one bar for every forty to fifty guests.

🌿 **Dance Floors**

Plan on three square feet per person for the dance floor.

❦ **Musicians**

Allow twenty square feet per instrument.

❦ **Tents**

Calculate on twenty square feet of floor space per person when estimating the size of tent you will need. This will give you breathing room, and guests and waitstaff will be able to easily move around. Anything less could be confining, especially in inclement weather.

❦ **Restroom Facilities**

Allow one bathroom for every seventy-five guests, but check fire marshal rules and regulations.

Each location comes with its own unique set of logistical challenges. For example, one facility could require extra staff because of the venue layout or equipment. At one wedding held in a private home, the dishwasher capacity was limited, and one caterer felt the need for extra staff as backup to manually wash dishes, cutlery, and glassware. The same caterer, in another location, might not have an issue. One venue may be union and another not, which could affect labor costs for moving in, setting up, tearing down, and moving out supplier requirements. A union facility will be very specific in what a company must do or provide to work in their venue including hours worked, break and meal times. This is true whether the entertainment setup crew is in-house (provided by the venue) or one you have brought in to handle your wedding entertainment.

Regardless of the venue, there are certain things that will need to take place in a specific order. Different suppliers will be handing off to one another—very much in the same way you would run a relay race—all depending, of course, on the wedding elements you are including. For example, if you are bringing in a stage and dance floor, it will need to be moved in and laid down before the tables and chairs are set and decorated. The supplier moving the tables into place will have to work closely with the lighting company if, for example, pinspotting of the tables will be required. Once the lighting is in place, the tables cannot be moved out of alignment or it will throw off the special effect. The florist can't set out the centerpieces until the décor company has finished dressing the dinner tables. If the stage and dance floor are scheduled to arrive after all this has taken place, you create planning pandemonium.

Once your options for your wedding ceremony and reception venues have been narrowed down, potential suppliers will be able to present you with an estimate based on specific sites and render you a more accurate idea of costs for which you will be responsible.

Wedding suppliers need to know what else is taking place in the room and how the timing is being worked out. If they are not asking the right questions, be wary. Somewhere down the line, you will be hit with an unexpected cost or glitch. Use your Wedding Vision sheets, Wedding Day Blueprint, and question-naires to guide you through the process, but look to work with suppliers that are on the ball, are supplying answers to you in advance of your questions, and are actively demonstrating a clear understanding of your vision, budget parameters, and logistical requirements. As you receive and review each wedding supplier's cost proposal, map out costs and requirements on your Wedding Day Blueprint in sequential order. This will give you a very clear picture of how your wedding needs to unfold.

Taking Good Care of You

Selecting the Right Wedding Vendors

WEDDING ORCHESTRATION REQUIRES operational insight in the planning and proposal and supplier quote stages, otherwise you will find that "estimated" costs go way over the line. You will be able to detect from the questions they ask, how they lay out your proposal, and the suggestions they put forth which vendors are the best equipped to deliver what you're looking for.

While you are contracting individual suppliers, each one of them has a domino effect on the others that can impact costs and what they will require. You need to obtain your wedding supplier and vendors' costs and requirements to complete the rest of your Wedding Blueprint cost breakdown so you can move into the contract phase with your wedding ceremony venue, reception site, and wedding suppliers. Completing your blueprint will allow you to make educated decisions you know you can live with. Being enlightened regarding total expenditures, and as to how those figures have been arrived at, enables you to contract with confidence.

Wedding planning can be divided into two separate areas. There is the creative side (right-brain thinking that is visual and processes information in an intuitive way, looking first at the whole picture and then the details), which is the mode you are in when designing your wedding vision, the foundation for your blueprint. Then there is the more linear side (left-brain thinking that is verbal and processes information in an analytical and sequential way, looking first at the pieces then putting them together to get the whole), which covers the critical wedding planning elements such as requests for quotes from suppliers, timing, logistics, strategy, financial considerations, negotiations, and contracting—the framework of your wedding.

As you move through the various steps, you are employing both right and left side of the brain thinking at different times. It is extremely important at this point in your wedding planning process not to lose your focus and get pulled away from doing what matters most when it matters most—which is left-brain thinking and more task-oriented. Right now, switching gears back into the more pleasurable aspects of creative design—for example, choosing to spend hours searching for the perfect wedding dress before you have identified all your wedding costs and contracted your wedding venues and suppliers—can throw you completely off your objective (orchestrating a wedding that meets your vision and your budget). You can easily estimate a total dollar amount you will spend on a dress, headpiece, veil, shoes, etc., pulling costs off the Internet, from bridal magazines, newspapers, bridal expos, or make a few quick calls—not visits—to bridal shops for price ranges.

In Steps 1, 2, and 3, you were working in a creative mode. Going forward in the planning steps (4, 5, and 6) has brought your into a more linear line of thinking and it is important for you to stay there. You must obtain all costs for all wedding elements that have been laid out in your Wedding Day Blueprint, so that you can finalize negotiations, secure venue and supplier services, and go to contract knowing all costs, terms, and conditions before swinging back into creative mode. Not finding your dress at this stage will not hold up contracting your wedding venues and suppliers, but not finishing the framework of costs that make up your Wedding Blueprint will. That is what you must stay focused on right now.

Wedding suppliers and vendors that fall under the planning framework category—whose costs and requirements it is essential to know before contracting with all your wedding venues and suppliers—include:

- Invitations and other printed material
- Transportation
- Décor
- Flowers
- Centerpieces
- Table tops, table settings, table and chair rentals
- Food and beverages
- Music and entertainment
- Photography
- Finishing touches
- Miscellaneous (insurance, permits, etc.)

Supplier's Information Worksheet

Fill in this worksheet and make copies to hand or fax to prospective suppliers.
Also check each section below for additional information specific suppliers may need.

- Wedding date _____
- Time and location of ceremony _____
  _____
- Time and location of reception _____
  _____
- Are floor plans available? _____
- When you will have access to the ceremony venue _____
- When you will have access to the reception venue _____
- What time guests will be arriving and departing _____
  _____
- What you envision taking place with regard to timing _____
  _____
- When you will have to be out _____
- Do the venues have any restrictions the supplier should know about? _____
  _____
- Contact person for ceremony venue _____
- Contact person for reception venue _____
- The number of guests (be sure to include suppliers and the wedding officiant in your count
  if appropriate for food and beverages, seating, etc.) _____
  _____
- Your budget _____
- Colors of ceremony venue _____
- Colors of reception venue _____
- Type and style of meal and beverage service _____
  _____

❧ Questions to Ask Prospective Suppliers

Make copies of this worksheet and fill it out as you interview prospective suppliers.
Also, check each applicable supplier section for additional questions on the following pages.

- What are their areas of expertise? _____

_____

- Have they won any awards in this area? _____
- How qualified are their staff? _____
- What type of client do they predominantly serve (e.g., corporate, social, wedding, other)?

_____

- What size of event do they generally handle? _____

_____

- How is their business run? Do they own their items, subcontract them, or custom create them for each client? _____

_____

- Are the items they bring in flame retardant and do they meet all fire and safety regulations?

_____

- What permits and insurance will they require? _____

_____

- What are their electrical requirements? _____

_____

- Do they know of or foresee any limitations in your selected venues, such as pre-wedding areas, storage, etc.? _____
- How long will it take them to move in and set up? _____

_____

- Do they have any special move-in and setup requirements? _____

_____

- How long will it take them to tear down and move out? _____

_____

- Do they have any special teardown and move-out requirements? _____

_____

- Will they be handling other events on your wedding day—both directly before and after—and if so, how tightly are they scheduled? _____

_____

- If teardown does not take place until all guests have departed, would this result in any overtime or other charges (e.g., for rental items)? _____

_____

Tips to Remember

- Make sure that all applicable taxes, service charges, and tips are laid out clearly for you in their quote. Find out exactly how their calculations will be billed to you at the time of final reconciliation (e.g., if the service charges and tipping are taxed as well as their fees, and on what amount each percentage is multiplied). GET THIS IN WRITING.
- Make sure that all delivery charges are included in the quote.
- Request that the number of people on the staff is listed and broken down by responsibility. Terms should include when and if overtime charges will apply and if there are any other special concessions you need to be made aware of, such as insurance and financial responsibility for missing or damaged items.
- In addition to written references, request phone numbers of three or four previous clients you can call.

Sources of Information

- The special event industry has an association called International Special Events Society (www.ises.com) that is highly regarded. On their website, they do have a section called "find an ISES member" and you can enter your region and type of supplier you are looking for.
- Check with your wedding ceremony site and reception venue to see if they have a preferred supplier list.
- Check with high-end hotels or restaurants in your area to ask who they use.

Invitations and Other Print Material

AT THIS TIME, your focus is on pricing and timing information with regard to your printed material so that you can incorporate the printing costs into your Wedding Day Blueprint and move forward with contracting your venues. The actual wording is best left until after all your wedding elements are in place—if you stop to work on it now, it will derail you. Once you have fully developed your wedding elements and contracted your venue and your suppliers, you will be in better position to design your print material to match your wedding inclusions.

Invitation and Other Print Material Options

There are three main ways to purchase your wedding invitation:

- Purchasing printed invitations
- Creating your own invitations
- Ordering invitations from a card shop, a printer, or a graphic design artist

How to Determine Your Requirements

You will need to decide exactly what you will be sending out. Your print material options may include:

- Save the date cards
- Wedding invitations
- Wedding insert cards (e.g., containing directions or other information)
- RSVP cards
- Place cards and place card assignment charts
- Menus
- Thank-you cards

You will need to consider:

- Your total guest count
- How many invitations you will actually be sending (taking into account couples and families)
- Include an extra invitation to mail to yourself when the rest go out so you can monitor the arrival date
- Whether you will be compiling A and B guest lists and will require additional invitations

- How many extra invitations you want on hand in case any addresses are incorrect, you spell a name wrong as you are addressing the cards, or you're having them prepared by a calligrapher, or to have a personal memento for your personal keepsake

- How many place cards you will require (consider whether you will have children attending and whether couples will be sitting together or apart)

- How many printed menus you will require (base your figures on one per person as couples may or may not be seated side by side depending on your seating preference)

- How many thank-you cards you will send out (include thank-you cards for engagement parties, bridal showers, bachelor/bachelorette party, wedding gifts, wedding venue, and suppliers)

- Whether your wedding invitations and RSVP cards will have a return address printed on them

- Whether you will require the services of a professional calligrapher or someone else to address your envelopes, or whether you will have the addresses formally printed

- Whether you will use the printing company to collate and stuff your invitations

- The difference in local and international postage rates for standard size and weight invitations versus oversize invitations

- Local and international delivery schedules and what the minimum and maximum number of days are for delivery

What Your Invitation Printing Company Will Need to Know

In addition to the Supplier's Information Worksheet, your invitation supplier will need to know:

- Your timelines—the dates by which you will require your print material (see the next section on timeline considerations)

- Type of print material you will be requiring (e.g., invitations, RSVP cards, number of enclosures, etc.)

- Quantities of each type required

- Quality of paper—if you are looking for stock or specialty paper, such as handmade, Japanese, vellum, watermark, torn edges (deckle edge), die cut (specialty shapes), and decorative envelope linings

- Type of printing—embossed (raised print), thermography (raised print that is similar in appearance to engraved printing, but less expensive and is adhered only to the surface with no impression; the back of the paper is smooth), engraved (formal and leaves an impression on the back of the paper), letterpress (more expensive), etc.

- Colors
- Fonts (typeface)
- Graphics

Invitation Timeline Considerations

- Guest list development should occur one year to eight months before your wedding. Allow a minimum of eight weeks to check guest list names and addresses.
- The invitation design should be completed eight to six months before your wedding date. The turnaround time for many printers is four weeks to produce a first review of invitation design.
- Your first review of invitation design should be proofed, signed off, and approved a minimum of six months before your wedding date.
- Second review of invitation design should be proofed, signed off, and approved (if applicable) one week after first invitation review.
- Envelopes should be addressed, stuffed, and a sample taken to the post office to be weighed to ensure correct postage is affixed. Allocate a minimum of two weeks to prepare your wedding invitations for mailing.
- Send out guest list A invitations twelve weeks prior to your wedding date. Keep in mind your legal room capacity. Your wedding ceremony and reception can be closed down if you exceed your maximum room capacity, which is set by fire regulations.
- Request guest list A RSVP eight to six weeks before your wedding date.
- Send out guest list B invitations (if applicable) eight to six weeks before your wedding date.
- Request guest list B RSVP a minimum of four weeks before your wedding date.

Important Invitation Mailing Considerations

- Local and international delivery schedules can affect your timelines.
- Consider busy holiday schedules such as Thanksgiving, the winter holiday season, school breaks, summer vacation, and when your guests may not be at home to receive your invitation.
- Print shops sometimes close for holidays.

🌸 The print shop workload can affect your invitation schedule. Can they guarantee that they can meet your proposed deadlines or will their existing workload cause delays?

🌸 Build in time buffers based on your personal work loads, home and wedding commitments, computer breakdowns, meeting attrition and cancellation dates for wedding venue and suppliers for guest count and food and beverage guarantees, and dates to finalize your seating chart and place cards. Keep in mind that you want to keep the last two weeks before your wedding day as free as possible.

Ask your invitation printing company for all applicable printing charges, including graphics, design layout, screening charges, taxes and service charges (and how they are calculated), rush fees, courier costs, etc., along with their timelines. What will they need from you, and by when, to meet your required dates?

What to Look For

🌸 Ask if you can receive your envelopes first so that you begin addressing them as soon as possible.

🌸 Find out the price difference if you order a larger quantity than you require. Sometimes with print material, it can actually cost the same or less to order more. If this is the case with your supplier, find out if the extra card stock (the amount in excess of what you truly need) can be given to you blank—not imprinted, which would only go to waste—so that you can use them for casual thank-you notes in the future.

🌸 Check to see if you will receive a discount if you place orders for your accompanying pieces such as place cards, menus, etc., with them.

What to Watch Out For

🌸 Traditionally, printing companies close during their scheduled vacation time. Some companies and graphic designers send their designs out to printing houses for fulfillment as opposed to doing the work in-house. Check to see if the company or the company they send their printing to will be closed at any time.

🌸 Printers can require four weeks or longer to fill orders. Make sure that you find out how long the process will take from the time of placing your order.

Special Considerations

- Be sure to package any specialty invitations in bubble envelopes or other protective packaging and take them to the post office to be hand stamped. This will also ensure sufficient postage and prompt delivery.

- Consider purchasing special issue postage stamps as opposed to more traditional ones. Check with your local post office to see what creative options are available to you.

- Your invitations set the tone of anticipation for your wedding. Your wedding invitations do not have to be expensive, but they should reflect the tone and your wedding vision style—whether formal or informal. Give some thought as to what is appropriate.

- Always, *always* have someone double check the proofs with you. Wedding invitations have been printed—after being proofed by the bride and groom—with errors in the wedding date, misspelled names, and the like. It is easy to skip quickly over what you are most familiar with. You have to take the time to proof your printed material word by word for spelling, dates, numbers, and alignment and have someone else do a double-check.

- If children are being invited to your wedding, their names are usually included on the invitation, clearly letting parents know they are invited. If they are not, just the invited guests' names should be on the invitation, letting the recipient know exactly who the invitation is intended for. If children are not being invited to attend, you need to plan how you will handle requests from guests wishing to bring their children.

Transportation

As you research transportation options, you'll need to consider all of these items and add any applicable costs to your blueprint.

- How will your guests be arriving at your wedding and getting to your wedding reception?
- Will they be making their own way? Will they be using public transportation or driving their cars?
- Will your guests be coming from work and be bringing two cars or coming together as a couple?
- Will they have designated drivers?

- Will you need to provide taxi fare for any guests who may have had too much to drink?

- Do you know how late public transportation and taxi service will be running at your reception site? This could impact your timing of events if your guests will need to slip away early to catch the last bus, train, or taxi home.

- Do both your venues have sufficient parking?

- Do you know the policy regarding street parking at both your venues? If you are getting married in the winter, what restrictions could apply regarding street parking and snow removal?

- Will you have to obtain and pay for any parking permits, valet parking, or shuttle transportation from site to site for your guests?

- Will you require traffic direction assistance and need to pay for an off-duty police officer?

- Will there be any heavy traffic due to construction, major events, or even normal rush hour flow?

- Will it be challenging to get from place to place and will you require a police escort?

- How will both of you be arriving at your wedding ceremony, your photo shoot location, your reception, and the location where you will be spending your wedding night?

- How will your wedding party be arriving at your ceremony, your wedding photo shoot, your reception, and back to their home again?

Work out your transportation logistics so that you will know exactly what you need, as well as where and when.

How to Determine Your Transportation Requirements

Map out your route and the number of vehicles and limousines you will need, along with a clear understanding of your timing so that the limousine company can give you an accurate cost. Limousines can be rented two ways: you can hire a limousine to be with you from beginning to end or hire limousines on a one-way transfer basis. The danger of renting a limousine on a one-way transfer basis is they can be held up in traffic going from job to job or be delayed if the transfer they are handling before you is running late. If you hire a limousine for a specific period of time, the same driver remains with you and if you need to leave earlier than planned, he or she is at your disposal.

What Your Limousine Company Will Need to Know

In addition to the Supplier Information Worksheet, your transportation provider will need to know:

- Location of your wedding photo shoot
- Location of your wedding reception
- How many people per limousine
- Pick-up locations and times for transfer to your wedding ceremony
- Pick-up locations and times for wedding shoot
- Pick-up locations and times for transfer to your wedding reception
- Pick-up times and location transfer to your drop-off points
- Whether you will require beverages to be available in each limousine
- The type of beverages you want your limousine to be stocked with

Questions to Ask Your Limousine Company

- How many limousines do they have similar in color and style?
- Can you reserve specific color and style of their vehicles for a visual impact if you require more than one (e.g., a whole row of the same color and style of limousine is visually more appealing than a mixture)?
- Do they have any classic limousines for hire?
- What is the seating configuration of the limousines they have to offer?
- How many people can the limousine comfortably hold?
- Are you charged from the moment the limousine leaves their company until it returns (called "barn to barn") or are you charged from your reserved pick-up and drop-off times?
- Will the limousine arrive clean and full of gas?
- Will your limousines be coming from another event and what would happen in the event of a delay on their part?
- Do you need to block and build in a time buffer?
- What would happen in the event of a mechanical failure—does the company have backup limousines available or are they a one-person or one-limousine operation?

Sources of Information

Check the limousine companies that service top business hotels and luxury resorts. You know that their drivers are professionally trained. Drive by a popular wedding photo site and view the limousines on display. Discreetly, if the bride and groom are away from their limousine having their photos taken, ask the driver for their company name or card. Do not ask them to let you see the interior of the limousine. You can do that on your site inspection if the vehicle and driver look as though they would meet your needs. To ask to see the inside when the bride and groom's personal effects may be in the car would be asking the driver to breach business ethics.

What to Look For
&sa; Drivers who are well groomed, polished, and professional
&sa; Limousines that gleam and show that they have been well tended

What to Watch Out For
&sa; Limousines that do not look well maintained

Special Considerations
Make sure that all applicable taxes, service charges, and tipping are laid out clearly for you. Find out exactly how their calculations will be billed to you at time of final reconciliation. For example, determine if you will be charged "barn to barn" charges or if you will be charged from your pick-up and drop-off points. Another example is to find out whether tipping is based on the base amount or on the total amount after taxes and service charges have been applied.

A FULL SERVICE décor company can handle all or part of your décor, floral, rental items such as props to coat racks, table settings, cutlery, glassware, tables, chairs, linens, overlays, chair covers, and lighting requirements. Some décor companies own their own props and have specialty divisions, such as their own in-house florist, while others subcontract what they need to bring in. Both have their pros and cons. With a décor company that owns their own props, you may be limited to using only what they can provide unless they are willing to look outside to find what you need to complement what they have in stock. On the other hand, they may offer a custom product that no one else can obtain. A décor company that subcontracts has the flexibility to work with a variety of suppliers and designers to create a look that is right for you. Your décor needs—how extensive and elaborate they are—will determine the best fit for you. You may prefer one-stop shopping by going through a full-service décor company or just using them for specific event elements and working directly with florists, rental companies, etc., for the rest if your design needs are not complex and you have the time and inclination to do so. The savings may not be major between the two ways of handling your décor requirements, but you may end up with a more pulled-together look working through one designer as opposed to pulling the pieces together yourself from different suppliers.

How to Determine Your Requirements

Your décor requirements will be determined by your wedding vision and your budget. Once you have added the costs of your wedding ceremony site rental, your reception venue charges, and food and beverage components to your Wedding Day Blueprint, the dollars you will have left to spend on items such as décor, flowers, music and entertainment, audiovisual, special lighting, photographer, etc., will emerge. Once you have an idea of the dollars you have left to spend, you can look at where they may be most effective and how they can work to best capture your wedding day must-haves.

What is important is to have the décor company lay everything out menu-style and detail what the décor costs would be at the wedding ceremony site and at the reception. You may need to scale one or the other back and you need to know how the décor dollars have been assigned—including delivery, labor, and staffing charges. Have your décor company present you with exactly what you need to put in place to be effective and break the add-ons into optional enhancements. You will have key decisions to make if dollars are becoming limited and you need to work with a décor company that has creative cost-saving ideas on how to achieve the look you want for less.

At the wedding ceremony, focus your décor dollars on what will be serving as a backdrop for your wedding photographs as opposed to blanketing the whole room if dollars are getting tight. Spend them where it will matter most and will have the most visual impact. For example, floral arrangements tied to the end of pews could easily get damaged as people are moving in and out, or become an item that can snag a wedding or bridesmaid's dress. They may not be noticeable in wedding photographs, and once your guests are seated, their attention is elsewhere. So unless the pew or chair floral décor is a must-have for you, they are an embellishment. Less expensive options, such as flowing ribbons, are preferable (but make sure that they are not long enough for anyone to trip on, or can easily come undone). Fresh rose petals scattered down the aisle, done for effect, can become slippery and hazardous for not just the wedding party, but the guests on exiting. Spend your décor dollars wisely.

Keep in mind that décor is one of your more fluid items. It can be molded to meet your budget requirements. If you can't afford to drape an entire room with fiber optics that are enhanced with theatrical lighting for dramatic effect, you may be able to include swags of fabric with twinkle lights, which, in the right décor company's hands, can create a similar illusion. Illusion is what décor is all about.

What Your Décor Company Will Need to Know

In addition to the Supplier's Information Worksheet, your décor provider will need to know the following information.

- Are floor plans of each venue available?
- What is the feeling you are looking to capture at your wedding ceremony?
- What is the mood and ambience you want your wedding reception to project?
- What is the interior of your wedding ceremony site like?
- What is your wedding color?
- What are the colors in the room at your wedding reception venue?
- How do you see your wedding ceremony unfolding?
- What will be taking place during your wedding reception?
- What type and style of meal and beverage service will you be providing?
- What else is taking place in the room?
- What is the room layout?
- What aspects of the décor would you like them to handle? Do you want them to handle room décor, table tops, table rentals, floral arrangements, centerpieces, lighting and special effects, etc., or just one or two event elements?

Questions to Ask Your Décor Company

- What specialty items do they recommend?
- Are they licensed to handle special effects, such as indoor fireworks? Will fire safety staff be a requirement of the fire marshal in order to include it? What additional costs do they need to factor in (e.g., fire marshal inspection, fire watch staff, permits, etc.)?
- What special effects and specialty items can they provide (e.g., indoor pyrotechnics, fiber optics, water walls, working water fountains, water dancing to music)?
- Do they create their own floral designs, have an in-house florist, or use the services of others?
- Do they only create room floral arrangements or can they design matching or complementary wedding party requirements as well (e.g., bridal bouquet,

bridesmaids' flowers, floral headpieces, boutonnieres, corsages, etc.)? If not, is there a florist they can recommend?

What to Look For

- ✿ Décor companies that will break down your cost menu-style and separate wedding ceremony décor costs from wedding reception costs.
- ✿ Companies that listen to your budget concerns, offering creative cost-cutting solutions, that will lay out exactly what you need in order to create the wedding vision you are going for, and will let you know what can be an optional enhancement for future budget consideration.
- ✿ Décor companies that offer new ideas using an old product.

What to Watch Out For

- ✿ Ask if they already own, will be subcontracting, or will be creating your design elements from scratch. If they will be custom creating items such as centerpieces or props for you, find out if at the end of the event they belong to you or what the price concessions are if they are keeping them, reusing them, and renting them out to other clients in the future. Some décor companies obtain their warehouse of items by creating custom goods for clients and then simply keeping them to rent out to new clients. The client has simply not thought to ask if they are being rented or purchased. Customized décor items can also serve a dual purpose and become take-home wedding favors or even become part of a bride and groom's home and entertaining décor. Maximize the benefits of the money you are spending.
- ✿ A supplier who will not do a site inspection of the venue if they have not done events in the facility before.

What to Expect and Inspect During Your Site Inspection

- ✿ Ask to see photos of their work and ask them specifically what they were responsible for in the photographs (e.g., they may have only done the centerpieces, but the photograph shows the entire room filled with décor).
- ✿ If they have their own warehouse of props and décor items, ask to see them so that you can judge the quality and how they are maintained (e.g., no cigarette burns, rips, stains, signs of visible mending, age, etc.).

Special Considerations

☙ Remember to put the focus on what can be seen—a good rule of thumb is from the waist up. Once your room is filled with guests—seated or standing—any dollars spent on décor or trimmings that have been positioned on or near the floor will be lost in a sea of bodies. You want the room to sparkle and for guests' eyes to be drawn upward. Visualize what guests will actually see when they have all arrived and are mingling and moving about the room.

☙ Make sure that all applicable taxes, service charges, and tips are laid out clearly for you. Find out exactly how their calculations will be billed to you at time of final reconciliation (e.g., if the service charges and tipping are taxed as well as the décor costs and on what amount each is multiplied).

☙ Make sure that all delivery charges are included in the quote.

☙ Request that the number of staff people is listed and broken down by responsibilities. Have the terms include when and if overtime charges would apply and if there are any other special concessions you need to be made aware of such as insurance and financial responsibility for missing or damaged items.

☙ Be sure that suppliers who may actually be seated with your guests (e.g., photographer, wedding officiant, etc.) are included in your guest count, as this could affect décor pricing on the number of tables, chairs, table tops, and table settings.

Floral Arrangements

WHAT WOULD A wedding be without flowers? Fresh flowers are an easy way to add color, warm up a room, and make a visual statement. You'll want to be as thoughtful and specific about your floral arrangements as about everything else in your wedding.

How to Determine Your Requirements

Keep in mind that during prime wedding season, flowers may be in great demand and, therefore, more expensive. You may wish to consider selecting just one color and one type of flower to create a sense of profuse abundance and to provide high visual impact. Check to see what other types of props your décor company or florist (or check local nurseries) may have available for rent, such as ficus trees with twinkle lights or tropical plants such as bougainvillea, hibiscus, magnolia, jasmine, gardenia, and orange trees, that may add something special to your setting.

What Your Floral Company or Floral Designer Will Need to Know

In addition to the Supplier Information Worksheet, your florist will need to know:

- ✿ The delivery locations
- ✿ The time of delivery
- ✿ What look you are envisioning
- ✿ The colors in the room and in your wedding décor (bring a sketch of the room layout and photos of your place setting, areas where you will be looking to create focal points, etc.)
- ✿ Table sizes—and for buffet tables what will be on it (colors and serving layout)—so they can recommend an appropriate design
- ✿ The color and style of your table covering, the china, silverware, and glassware
- ✿ Which floral arrangements they will handle—only room floral arrangements at the ceremony, the reception, or both, your bridal bouquet, flowers for your wedding party, etc.
- ✿ Your budget

What to Ask Your Floral Company or Floral Designer

- ✿ Do they have photographs of arrangements they have actually done—not stock photos of possible displays?
- ✿ Can they prepare a sample arrangement for you to see (that you will be required to pay for)?
- ✿ Will their staff be merely delivering the items to the venues or assisting with display setup?
- ✿ What is their policy on substitution?
- ✿ When will the flowers be at their peak—opened for maximum effect—and how does that fit with the timing of your event?
- ✿ How hardy are the flowers they are suggesting? Will they bruise easily? Are they long-lasting?
- ✿ How strong is their scent?
- ✿ Will you own the floral display and containers or do the containers need to be returned?
- ✿ Do they know of or foresee any décor or service limitations in your selected venues such as prep areas and tables, storage, refrigeration, etc.?
- ✿ Do their drivers have cell phones and do they provide emergency numbers?

Sources of Information

Check with quality hotels and restaurants to find out who does their floral displays. You want to work with florists who are creative and can produce floral arrangements that do not wilt quickly.

What to Look For

🙠 Florists who will break down your costs menu-style and separate wedding ceremony floral costs from wedding reception costs.

🙠 Floral designers who offer creative suggestions that are cost-saving or interesting alternatives. (For example, for a fall wedding they may suggest going with arrangements that feature Leonidas, often referred to as "Chocolate Roses." They originate in South America and offer wonderful color combinations that can range from rich cinnamon/burnt orange tones with a creamy yellow reverse to ochre/rosy-brown. The rose is lightly fragrant and will not be distracting when used as a table centerpiece. When fully opened the rose is approximately 4 inches across, but the arrangements show best when the roses are opened only halfway.)

What to Watch Out For

🙠 Florists who are trying to sell you more than you require. (For example, floral arrangements are never recommended for the bar area, as they only hinder bar service and bartenders generally tend to move them out of the way. Florists who suggest this may not be well schooled in handling special events, or may be interested in what they can sell you and not in selling you only what will have value to you.)

🙠 Find out from the florist if there are any special requirements you need to be aware of. (For example, after the flowers are delivered, what care will they require? Will the arrangements need to be refrigerated to prevent them from opening prematurely? How long can the flowers be expected to last?)

Centerpieces

CENTERPIECES CAN BE floral, candelabras, something unique, a mixture of elements, or even edible. One couple who married in the fall had apples covered in caramel and drizzled with chocolate set out on deep brown linens as part of their centerpiece display, with clear cellophane bags at each place setting so that their guests could take home a sweet reminder of their wedding to enjoy at their leisure. Centerpieces are typically handled by your décor company or florist—who may be the same or two separate companies handling different design elements. Sometimes centerpieces are created by a specialty shop. Regardless of who will be handling your centerpiece requirements, they will be asking you the same questions that would apply for floral arrangements.

If you are having a sit-down dinner, make sure that your centerpieces are low enough so that guests can see each other across the table, set on high pedestals that do not block the view from across the table, or hung from the ceiling above each table for an entirely different effect. Watch out that trailing ivy does not block the view when using high pedestals or spill all over the table top and take up excessive space.

Discuss unusual options that will fit your wedding vision and that are new and fresh. As you begin to finalize the number of guests you are planning to invite, keep an eye on the number of tables you will be requiring centerpieces for. As your count goes up and down and your table assignments change in size, it may be necessary to add or subtract centerpieces.

Table Tops, Table Settings, and Table and Chair Rentals

Use your imagination when it comes to tablecloths, overlays, table runners, and napkins. The range of fabrics and products out there is worth investigating. Tablecloths, overlays, table runners, and napkins can also be custom designed and embroidered or beaded to match your wedding gown. It is key that whoever is making them for you or has made the ones to rent has used specialty needles that have been designed to prevent puckering. Check to make sure that the fabric being used has been treated and is flame-retardant and stain-proof. If you are having table coverings made, check to see if any party companies would like to purchase them from you after your event. Depending on the quantities being ordered, this may be of interest to them and you will recover some of your costs.

Table tops (the look of the table including centerpieces), table settings (china, crystal, silverware), and table and chair rentals can be handled by your décor company, florist, caterer, in some cases by your venue, or by a rental company that can handle all or part of your requests but that may not be proficient in design. What you want to avoid is having the design elements appear disjointed or mismatched. It is not just the look that you have to factor in, but who will physically be unloading, taking inventory, making sure there are no damaged goods that need to be replaced, putting each piece on the table with skill and precision, collecting the items, repackaging them, and moving them out. If, for example, you have ordered table settings through your décor company, which staff will be clearing the dirty plates, cutlery, and glasses? Which staff will be responsible for rinsing them, washing them, and reloading them? This can be an area that is easily overlooked and you do not want to find yourself in the middle of your wedding with stacks of dirty dishes and no one accepting responsibility for them, or without critical serving components because one supplier thought the other was bringing them. The same applies at your wedding ceremony site if rental chairs are being brought in. Who will be setting them in place and packing them up for return delivery?

How to Determine Your Requirements

Your first step is to determine who already has what you will be using and where the missing pieces are. Look at your list and determine which type of supplier best fits your needs for what still has to be rented. Which wedding vendor has both the skills and the staff to do the job? Some wedding suppliers, in the hopes of securing a bigger piece of the business, allude to having done more than they really are qualified to do. They may simply be florists who aspire to be décor companies and at present do not have the resources they truly need to handle areas outside their realm or who will be subcontracting the services of a third party. You need to interview your suppliers to find out where each of their strengths are.

What Your Table Top, Table Setting, and Table and Chair Rental Company Needs to Know

In addition to the Supplier Information Worksheet, your rental company will need to know:

- What feeling, mood, and ambience you are looking to capture at your wedding ceremony and reception
- What the interior of your wedding ceremony site is like
- Your wedding color theme
- The colors in the room at your wedding reception venue
- How you see your wedding ceremony unfolding
- What will be taking place during your wedding reception
- What type and style of meal and beverage service you will be providing
- The number of guests you are expecting

- What else will be going on in the room
- The room layout
- What aspects you would like them to handle—table top décor, table settings, table and chair rentals, etc., or just one or two event elements

Questions to Ask Your Table Top, Table Setting, and Table and Chair Rental Company

- What specialty items do they recommend?
- What items can they provide?
- Given your guest count and number of tables, what quantities do they recommend you order? (You are looking for suppliers who know to recommend more than one glass, napkin, etc., per person, regardless if you are doing a buffet or plated dinner. For example, extra napkins and silverware will be required to replace soiled or dropped guest napkins and should be recommended. Experienced companies will do this as a matter of course and it is a good cross-check as to the caliber of the supplier you are considering.)
- Do they create their own floral designs, have an in-house florist, or use the services of others?
- Do they just do room floral arrangements or can they design matching or complementary wedding party requirements as well (e.g., bridal bouquet, bridesmaids' flowers, floral headpieces, boutonnieres, corsages, etc.)? If not, is there a florist they can recommend?
- Do they know of or foresee any décor or service limitations in your selected venues such as prep areas, storage, layout restrictions (e.g., table count if any of your guests are disabled and in wheelchairs and will need extra space between the tables to maneuver around, etc.)?

What to Look For

- Companies that will break down your costs menu-style and separate wedding ceremony requirement costs from wedding reception costs.
- Companies who listen to your budget concerns, offering creative cost-cutting solutions and that will lay out exactly what you need in order to create the wedding vision you are going for, companies that will let you know what can be an optional enhancement for future budget consideration—items that are nonessential and with or without them your wedding design will stand on its own.

What to Watch Out For

- Ask if they already own, will be subcontracting, or will be creating your design elements from scratch. If they will be custom creating items such as centerpieces or props for you, find out if at the end of the event they belong to you, or what the price concessions are if they are keeping them, reusing them, and renting them out to other clients in the future. Look for items that can also serve a dual purpose and become take-home wedding favors or even become part of your entertaining and décor. Remember to always maximize the benefits of the money you are spending.

- A supplier that will not do a site inspection of the venue if they have not done events in the facility before.

What to Expect and Inspect During Your Site Inspection

- Take the time to visit with the company that will be handling your rentals. Make sure that their linens, chair covers, china, crystal, silverware, etc., are in good condition and are of the quality that you are looking for.

- When renting table rounds, make sure that the tables they are sending are a solid unit in the size requested and not plywood placed over a smaller table, as the plywood could easily tip if someone leans on it. New on the market are hydraulic tables that convert from 30-inch dining tables to 22-inch cocktail tables at the touch of a button.

Food

DO NOT FEEL as though you are limited to the items on the suggested menus the caterer or facility provides. Many food suppliers are happy to create a custom menu for you based on your budget as long as it meets their minimum pricing policies. Keep in mind the season, as seasonal food choices will be both more appropriate and more economical.

How to Determine Your Reception Requirements

Your food choices will depend on what you decide to do for your reception. Depending on the number of guests you're having and the formality of your wedding, you may choose to have a classic wine and cheese reception, cocktails and *hors d'oeuvres*, a cocktail reception followed by a sit-down or buffet dinner, or a dessert reception. Again, you are not bound by tradition. Feel free to include family favorites, foods that are meaningful to you and your groom, or food choices that accommodate the needs of your guests.

℘ Reception Considerations

- Plan on serving an assortment of no more than eight to ten appetizer items and calculate on each guest eating two to three of each if there is no meal to follow (a good rule of thumb for budget purposes is to base it on twenty-four pieces per person). Your caterer and banquet planning staff often refers to this as "heavy hot and cold *hors d'oeuvres.*" The amount required will vary depending on the length of your reception. Compare these costs to the cost of a buffet. In some venues, a buffet cost will be lower; but keep in mind that a buffet projects a different feeling from a lavish serving of appetizers, elegantly displayed, and passed on silver trays.
- If a meal is to follow, base your estimates on guests eating six to eight pieces per person.
- A feeling of lavish abundance is projected if you display only one type of appetizer on each circulating serving tray.
- Set up multiple mini tasting stations where guests can easily help themselves to the less expensive choices. Space them so that congestion is lessened, doorways are not blocked, and access to service areas is not compromised. If you put the more costly items out, they can disappear in a second and there is no way to control the number of pieces someone is putting on their plate. Having them passed gives you a measure of control and flow. Make sure that each station is set with plates, appropriate cutlery, and napkins.
- Use your imagination when it comes to your selection of appetizers and talk to your food service provider about innovative options within your budget.

Buffet Reception and Dinner Considerations

℘ When selecting menu items for your buffet, keep in mind what needs to be served hot, what needs to be kept cold, and what will taste good at room temperature.

℘ Do not duplicate items from your appetizer selection. If you have already served a shrimp dish, do not repeat it.

℘ Will the food items you are considering hold up well in a buffet? Can they be safely left out and, if so, for how long?

℘ Remember that hard cheeses dry out and can be difficult to cut. Softer cheeses such as Brie, Camembert, and goat cheese are better choices.

- Your buffet can feature one to two main entrees with a selection of side dishes. Quality and abundance is key, not unlimited choices. Be sure to include some vegetarian choices, and remember not all vegetarians eat dairy, so cheese toppings should be on the side.
- Include one extravagant item or display for the *wow* factor. A whole poached salmon, elaborate sushi display, or a mountain of lush oversized berries with fresh whipped cream will stand out. It does not have to be expensive to look extravagant.
- Make sure that your room is laid out so that your buffet tables can be accessed from both sides. Having staff on hand to help serve guests will aid in containing portion control so that there will be plenty for all guests.
- Make sure that your food supplier provides height variation on the buffet table. This can be easily done using milk crates and sturdy wooden boxes turned upside down and covered in draping.
- Wait staff will be needed to clear the dishes between visits to the buffet table.
- Plan and budget for additional plates, cutlery, and napkins to be used each time your guests visit the buffet table as they will be requiring a fresh set.

Stand-Up Buffet

- If your buffet will be stand-up, make sure that the portions are manageable and will not require the use of a knife. Serve slices of roast beef, turkey, or ham, for example, tucked into a roll, a small pita, or on a thin slice of specialty bread.
- Napkins and cutlery will need to be prewrapped.
- Salad plates will be more manageable than full-size dinner plates.

Sit-Down Buffet

- Consider having your first course—such as your appetizer, soup or salad—plated. Your guests can be seated and served their first course before lining up, then tables can be called to approach the buffet. This way you will avoid congestion and long lineups and your guests waiting their turn will have had something to eat.
- Make sure that there is sufficient space between tables so that your guests will be able to move about with ease.

Sit-Down Dinner Styles

- Plated—everything comes to the table on a plate
- French—your courses are served to your dinner plate by your waiter
- Family—courses are served to the table, set out on platters, and guests help themselves

Food Considerations When Children Are Attending Your Wedding

- Have child-friendly food available in easy-to-manage portions, such as mini hamburgers, hot dogs, pizza, macaroni, fresh fruit, and cookies. Do not include food that contains peanut butter or nuts as many children have allergies. Have milk and fruit punch available.
- If the children and their parents who are attending your wedding are comfortable with not being seated together, you could consider having a separate food table and play area for children in the same room under the supervision of babysitters.
- Make sure that alcoholic beverages are not left unattended or in reach of little hands. One or two ounces can be harmful for a toddler. Be mindful of serving chocolates with liqueurs in them.
- Make sure none of the prepared food items have toothpicks in them. They are a major cause of injury to small children. Hard candy and balloons can also be dangerous.
- Consider what needs to be in place for sleepy babies, toddlers, and young children. Safety-approved high chairs, booster seats, and playpens may be required.
- Serve the children first.
- Remember to include children in the count if you are giving out wedding favors and take the time to have their name on it to avoid conflict.

What Your Food Supplier Will Need to Know

In addition to the Supplier's Information Worksheet, your food supplier will need to know:

- What will be required in the way of food service and serving styles (e.g., tables of eight or ten, stand-up, etc.).
- Whether you have any special meal requirements.

Questions to Ask Your Food Supplier

- Ask them to detail what their staff will be responsible for. Will they be serving, taking drink orders, replenishing food items and clearing the tables, taking care of all cleanup, garbage disposal, and dishwashing?
- How many staff people at what levels of service will they be providing (e.g., one waitstaff per two tables for informal casual dining, etc.)?
- What size group are they best suited to cook for?
- Who is their clientele? Do they handle mainly weddings, corporate, or social events?
- Can they create a menu to fit your budget?
- Can they prepare a sample tasting (that you may be required to pay for)?
- If they are providing the tableware and glassware, how many plates, etc., per person are they providing? Ask to see them so you can judge the quality, and find out if this amount is separate from the bar requirements. At one wedding reception, the bar ran short of glasses because the catering company decided to use some of their supply to serve dessert.
- What additional items could be required to be brought in and at what cost?
- How fast are they at dishwashing turnaround?
- Ask where the food will be prepared. Will it be cooked off-site at their facilities and finished at the reception site or prepared on location?
- Find out how closely they book their functions. Will you be their only function on your wedding day or will they be rushing to or from another event?
- Are they licensed by the state health department (a must for guest safety)?

What to Look For

When selecting your menu, keep the following tips in mind:

- Food should be plentiful. Plan to have more than enough.
- Canapés should be bite sized, easy to handle, with no messy sauces or bits to get rid of such as shrimp tails, lamb or chicken bones, or skewers. When choosing your canapés, consider whether small plates are being provided or just napkins.
- Always include vegetarian choices.
- Avoid selecting items with peanuts or prepared with peanut oil due to high sensitivity in some guests.
- The menu should be easy to prepare and require a minimum of last-minute cooking in case the timing of serving your meal needs to be moved up or slowed down.

❧ The food should be pleasing to look at—whether you are serving a plated meal or buffet. Think presentation—visual impact. Look for variety in color, texture, and taste.

❧ From beginning to end, make sure that your food and drink selections complement each other.

❧ Your menu choices should include food high in protein—cheese, fish, and meat—and high in starches, which help to slow down the absorption of alcohol.

❧ If you are serving a buffet, make sure that your choices complement each other and that you have covered all areas.

❧ Decadent desserts are wonderful, but if you are also serving wedding cake, a lighter dessert made from fresh fruit may be a better choice. It will not take anything away from your wedding cake creation.

❧ Make sure that your wedding day is not the day your caterer or the in-house chef at your reception venue is considering using a new recipe without having mastered it (e.g., if you are having them prepare a family favorite).

❧ While it is tempting to include items that are reflective of current food trends in your menu selections, make sure that wherever possible for a main entrée that the spices are toned down. If you are serving an entrée where the sauce could be questionable, have it served on the side. A better time to introduce specialty items is as part of the *hors d'oeuvres* selection or as part of a buffet. That way guests will have alternate choices if they find the fare too hot to handle.

❧ Be sure to include suppliers you may be providing food for in your food guarantees (e.g., photographer, wedding officiant, etc.).

What to Watch Out For

❧ Be aware of food pricing. Are the food rates current and will you be subject to any increases that are in effect at the time your wedding takes place?

❧ What pricing buffer (e.g., 10 percent) do they recommend adding in to protect you from exceeding your budget?

❧ A supplier who will not do a site inspection of the venue if they have not done events in the facility before.

 Beverages

COSTS FOR BEVERAGES can either skyrocket or be carefully contained. Prices of champagne, wine and beer, or hard liquor vary a great deal, but it is usually possible to find quality beverages that cost a little less.

How to Determine Your Requirements

Of course, your beverage requirements are going to depend on how many guests you're having and what type of reception you're having, but they're going to depend on the discernment of your guests, as well. Your choices and costs will be different if yours is a family of wine connoisseurs, martini drinkers, or imported beer lovers. Aside from the traditional champagne, don't feel constrained—design your beverage choices to please yourselves and your loved ones.

  Choosing Your Champagne
Guide to Champagne
- Brut—Extra dry
- Extra sec or sec—Medium dry to medium sweet
- Demi sec or doux—Sweet to very sweet

Keep in mind these measures:
- 750 ml = Six (6) Flute Glasses of Champagne
- 1500 ml = Twelve (12) Flute Glasses of Champagne

  Calculate and budget on serving two glasses of champagne per person if waitstaff are pouring the glasses of champagne and topping them off. For fifty guests, estimate nine 1500 ml bottles of champagne.

  If you want to contain costs, one glass of champagne per guest can be served on polished silver trays by waitstaff—which is in itself a nice presentation—and do not have waitstaff circling to refill glasses.

  For a more dramatic presentation with added flair, have a parade of the "big bottles" by waitstaff who are proficient at carrying and pouring from oversized bottles. This serving style can add a bigger impact and bring a more festive feel to your wedding celebratory toasts:

- Magnum—equal to two single bottles
- Jeroboam—equal to four single bottles
- Rehoboam—equal to six single bottles
- Methuselah—equal to eight single bottles
- Salmanazar—equal to twelve single bottles
- Balthazar—equal to sixteen single bottles
- Nebuchadnezzar—equal to twenty single bottles

❧ Serve Champagne at 70 degrees Fahrenheit.

❧ Champagne should be stored in a cool, dark, quiet spot away from the kitchen and heat. Ensure that the champagne will be served well chilled. Gas causes the champagne cork to shoot out sooner than expected. If the champagne has been properly chilled, the gas expansion in the bottle will be reduced.

❧ Find out how your beverage provider will be chilling your champagne. Not all venues provide proper storage and chilling space. Champagne can be chilled in approximately twenty minutes in ice water, but that will cause the labels to become damaged or come off. Unopened bottles with the seal intact but with damaged labels will not be able to be refunded. Bottles set in ice take approximately two hours to properly chill. Bottles chill faster in crushed ice than in ice cubes. A suggestion to protect the labels from damage would be to slip each bottle into a clear plastic bag before they are put on ice. There are digital thermometers available that wrap around the outside of a bottle that will assist in knowing when your champagne is ready to be served.

❧ **Choosing Your Wines**
Sugar Content
- Very Dry—0 percent
- Dry—1 to 2 percent
- Medium—3 to 6 percent
- Sweet—7+ percent

Keep in mind these measures:
- 750 ml = Six 4-ounce servings
- 1500 ml = Twelve 4-ounce servings

❧ Calculate and budget on serving two glasses of wine per person, per hour. This should provide you with a beverage budget buffer.

❦ Serve light fruity red wines such as Beaujolais and rosé at 58 to 60 degrees Fahrenheit. Red wines are best served at cool room temperature (62 to 65 degrees Fahrenheit) with the cork removed to allow time to breathe.

❦ Calculate and budget on serving half a bottle of wine per person if you are serving cocktails before or during meal service. If you are serving only wine with the meal and waitstaff are pouring the glasses of wine and topping them off or leaving the bottle on the table for guests to help themselves, for budgeting purposes calculate on three quarters to one bottle of wine per person depending on the length of the reception.

❦ **Choosing Your Beers**
Include a mix of light, dark, imported, and nonalcoholic beers. You may want to see if a local brewery has a beer that would be something different or special. The choices in beer have expanded greatly in recent years, so you may want to taste a few yourselves before choosing your mix.

What Your Beverage Company Needs to Know

❦ What you envision taking place with regards to timing.

❦ What type of bar setup you will be requiring for your reception or premeal reception and brunch, lunch, or dinner:
- Wine and beer only
- Wine, beer, and specialty drinks
- Open bar (wine, beer, spirits)
- Wine with brunch/lunch/dinner following cocktails
- Wine with brunch/lunch/dinner (no premeal drinks)
- Champagne toast
- After-dinner liqueurs

Tip: Instead of serving liqueurs to their guests to enjoy with their coffee, one couple decided to do something a little different and create something that served the purpose. Chocolate-coated, liqueur-flavored spoons (cellophane wrapped and tied with a custom ribbon) were both memorable and cost less money.

❦ The breakdown of wine to be served (e.g., 60 percent white and 40 percent red). (This will vary based on menu choices and your guests' personal preference. Consumption of red wine is increasing and has often gone as high as 60 percent.)

- Whether you will want your bar costs based on consumption or on a negotiated flat rate. (If you are basing your bar costs on consumption, you will be charged for what your guests consumed. What you need to find out before you make a decision is whether or not you will be charged for the full cost of bottles of liquor or wine that are only partially consumed or just on the drinks that the guests have been served. A negotiated flat rate is one where you are charged a per person price, per hour for unlimited drinks.)
- Whether you want standard or premium brands to be served.
- Whether you want your guests to line up for their drinks, have drinks passed, or both during cocktails.
- Whether you want wine poured at the table or bottles placed on each table.
- Whether you will be offering guests additional wine (e.g., waiters topping up their glasses or bringing additional bottles of wine to the table).
- Whether you want the bar to remain open during the meal service or just have wine available. (Will beer, soft drinks, iced tea, lemonade, etc., be an included option for those who do not want to drink wine during the meal?)
- Will you require the waitstaff to take drink orders?
- Who will be providing staff for clearing—the food provider or the beverage provider (could be the same)?
- Whether you or the venue will be providing rental items such as cocktail tables, cruiser tables, scattered seating in the reception area, or whether you want them to handle these arrangements?
- Whether you require any specialty beverages such as specific vintage wines or mixers such as Clamato juice.
- Whether you want to serve any specialty drinks that will require any special glassware such as shooters or martinis.
- If you are having a champagne toast, will the champagne be poured and passed by waitstaff in flutes, poured at the table, or will individual mini champagne bottles be required at each place setting with or without a champagne flute (straws)?
- What will be taking place (activities) and in place (set up and furniture wise) in the room? (Walk them through the room layout and leave a copy for them.)
- A contact name at the facility and any other applicable supplier (e.g., food supplier).
- When guests will be departing.
- When they have to be out of the facility.
- Your budget.

Questions to Ask Your Beverage Company

- Will special permits be required to bring liquor into your chosen venue?
- What host and supplier liability insurance will be required?
- How will they ensure that you do not run out of beverages if you are paying for an open bar and they are bringing all supplies in?
- If they are providing the glassware, how many glasses and what style, per person, are they providing? Ask to see samples.
- Will they be providing napkins, bartending equipment, the bars, etc?
- What quality of garnishes, ingredients, and mixers will they be providing? Using quality ingredients is a tangible difference. It tells your guests that you care, demonstrates attention to detail, and elevates your bar into being its best. Lush olives; vibrant lemon, lime, and orange twists; freshly ground exotic spices; and creative garnishes are all visual enhancements that complement your bar setup. Whenever possible, use fresh squeezed juices. The taste of fresh juice is incomparable.
- What additional items could be required to be brought in and at what cost?
- How fast is their dishwashing turnaround?
- Are there any surcharges if you decide to have a bar based on consumption and your guests do not drink very much? Will there be a charge if you do not meet a minimum bar dollar amount?
- Will special permits be required to extend bar hours past normal close-down times?
- What is their policy on serving guests who drink a little too freely?
- Can they advise an appointed member of your wedding party when liquor consumption has reached your halfway budget point so that a decision can be made to slow down service or close the bars earlier than anticipated?
- If you are bringing alcohol into the venue, will the venue be charging your beverage supplier a corkage charge that you will need to add into your budget?
- What is their return policy on unopened bottles?
- What new products or drinks do they recommend?
- What new specialty bars do they suggest?
- Will they be preparing any specialty drinks that require ice or crushed ice? How will that affect service time at the bar and what will you require from the venue in order to facilitate your ice supply and electrical requirements?

What to Look For

❧ In order to avoid areas of congestion and long lineups at the bar, you will need to have a number of bars set up in various locations. Estimate one bar station per forty to fifty guests with one bartender serving no more than forty guests. Find out the number of bars your quote will be based on and where they see them being positioned on your venue room layout.

❧ Double bar setups, where two bars are located side by side, depending on room layout, congestion, and number of guests, should be manned by three bartenders (two to tend bar and one to pour wine, soft drinks, etc., for waiters). Look for areas of congestion or bottlenecks on your room layout if this is your supplier's recommendation.

❧ Make sure each bar station is fully stocked and that the bars are manned by professional bartending staff who have at least six months of training. Find out the quantity and quality of staff they will be guaranteeing (as a clause in your contract) to provide.

What to Watch Out For

❧ Are the beverage rates current and will you be subject to any increases that are in effect at the time your wedding takes place?

❧ What pricing buffer (e.g., 10 percent) do they recommend adding in to protect you from exceeding your budget?

❧ How will minors at your wedding (if applicable) be handled if they request an alcoholic beverage?

❧ Check out their policy on tipping. Tip jars placed on bars should not be permitted.

❧ Remember to include some nonalcoholic champagne and beverages.

Quick Stats and Facts

❧ One bar for every forty to fifty guests.

❧ One bartender for every forty guests.

❧ Minimum of three glasses per person for the bar.

❧ Estimated two drinks per person per hour for budgeting purposes.

❧ The white to red wine ratio should be 60/40 (this could change depending on your family and friends' personal preferences).

❧ Estimate on one-half to one bottle of wine per person for budgeting purposes (this will depend on whether other drinks will be served).

❧ Two glasses of champagne per person for toasts.

Rentals

YOUR RENTAL REQUIREMENTS will be based on what you will need to supply that is not being provided by your wedding ceremony site, wedding reception venue, caterers, beverage providers (caterers can do both food and beverage), décor company, florist, entertainment, audiovisual, staging, and lighting companies.

How to Determine Your Requirements

Your first step is finding out what is still missing, if you are happy with the quality of what is being provided, or if it needs upgrading. For example, in the case of hotel ballroom chairs, you may want to bring in something a little more upscale or use the existing chairs with chair covers from a specialty rental company or your décor company to give them a different look. You may want to begin by inquiring whether one of your other suppliers can provide items that you need. For instance, your caterer or décor company may also be able to provide rental items such as coat racks and hangers, as well as experienced staff. It means one less delivery and item to keep track of, but whether or not that is feasible will depend on how much more it will cost or if it is a specialty item. In some cases your suppliers' costs could be comparable to what you could do on your own because they are working with these suppliers year-round and can sometimes receive a volume discount.

What Your Rental Company Will Need to Know

In addition to the Supplier's Information Worksheet, your rental company will need to know:

- ❧ Rental dates—how long you will need the item
- ❧ Delivery addresses and special instructions
- ❧ What time items need to be picked up

Questions to Ask Your Rental Company

- ❧ Ask exactly what services they will be supplying. Will they merely be delivering the items to you, or will they be setting them up in position and tearing them down as well?
- ❧ Are the items insured against theft or damage?
- ❧ What insurance will you or your facility need to have in place?

Sources of Information

> Antique shops are often amenable to renting furniture and accessory items. Be sure to discuss rental costs, delivery charges, and insurance with them.

What to Look For

> Really inspect the quality of the items they are supplying.

What to Watch Out For

> Look at how many layers of markup will come into play if you do your rental items through your décor company, caterer, or the like. You will have to weigh the cost versus your time. Sometimes it makes better sense to have as many items under one umbrella. What you have to keep in mind is that many suppliers subcontract with others so instead of one mark-up fee, you could be paying two or three on the same item.

> Watch out for additional unforeseen costs, such as labor. If, for example, you decide to bring in a different style of chair through a rental agency as opposed to your décor company, their only responsibility may be getting the chairs delivered to your site. The cost for labor to move the chairs in, place them in position, collect them at the end of the evening, and get them ready for pickup is not included. The facility you are using may not let their crew in to set up and you must obtain staff from the facility to do it for you. Always make sure setup and teardown are accounted for.

Special Considerations

> When it comes to chasing individual items like booster seats, high chairs, water fountains, dance floors, etc., really consider whether the cost savings will be worth it. If, for example, your décor company takes on sourcing a dance floor for you, they will also be taking on the on-site orchestration of making sure it is in place before they move all that they need to.

Music and Entertainment

MUSIC MUST BE planned. It is an important ingredient in setting a mood. You have endless choices—live entertainment, high energy bands, symphony or glass orchestras, disc jockeys, and jukeboxes. The music played at your wedding ceremony does not have to set the tone for your wedding reception. One can be soft and romantic and the other a joyous celebration. Consider all of your musical opportunities, such as guest arrival, pre-ceremony as guests wait, during the wedding, post-ceremony, and at your reception.

What Your Musicians and Entertainment Company Need to Know

In addition to the Supplier's Information Worksheet, your entertainment company will need to know:

- Whether you are considering having them play at both the ceremony and the reception or just one or the other
- The age group of your guests
- Whether there will be dancing
- The feeling you are looking to capture at your wedding ceremony
- The mood and ambience you want your wedding reception to project
- What the interior of your wedding ceremony site is like
- Your wedding color theme
- How you want them to dress
- Your musical and entertainment needs
- How you see your wedding ceremony unfolding
- What will be taking place during your wedding reception
- What type of music you want played
- What other music or entertainment will be taking place
- The room layout
- Whether they will be performing on a stage and, if so, the dimensions
- Whether there are any noise restrictions they have to comply with

Questions to Ask Your Musicians and Entertainment Company

- What are your power needs?
- Will you be providing your own sound system?
- Are there any special requirements you may have (e.g., such as a piano tuner) that may need to be factored into your budget?
- What do you require for a smooth move in and setup?
- What time would you be setting up at our wedding ceremony and/or reception?
- Will you be doing a rehearsal and require rehearsal time blocked?
- When will you be doing a sound check?
- Would you be performing somewhere else prior to coming to our wedding?
- Would you be performing somewhere else immediately after our wedding?

- What equipment will you require us to provide (e.g., a disc jockey may require a draped table and chair)?
- What are the terms of your technical rider (e.g., dressing rooms, staging, lighting, travel, and meal provisions)?
- Ask them for their song list and have your list prepared before you speak with them.
- Can you handle special musical requests?
- What do you typically wear to perform?
- How far in advance of the start time will your musicians be at our wedding ceremony and/or reception site?

Tip: It is advisable to schedule the music to begin playing at least fifteen minutes before your actual start time to ensure that all musicians are in place and ready to go well in advance of when you want the music to commence.

- How long are your sets and what is your break schedule?
- What do we need to put in place so that when you take your breaks there is no dead air?
- Do you do encores? (These have to be negotiated as part of your contracts.)
- Is there anything in your act that would require fire marshal approval and permits, such as the use of pyrotechnics?
- Are you bringing in anything that requires fire retardant certification?
- Do you have insurance?

Sources of Information

- Entertainment management companies, talent agencies, and schools of music are sources to consider when looking for musical performers. An entertainment company will charge a management fee, but it is well worth the cost. They are on top of which performers are a perfect fit for a specific event, they know who will show up on time, put on a great show, and be able to keep your guests entertained. They also send a representative from their company to oversee the move in and setup and to make sure all goes as planned. There may be an additional charge for this but it is recommended if you want polished and professional acts performing at your weddings who will not cross any protocol or behavioral boundaries.

What to Look For

🙠 You need to know the overall look and sound the band or musicians are going to convey. The condition of their instruments is critical. Ask for photos of them and a recording of their music (preferably live).

What to Watch Out For

🙠 Make sure that you audition your entertainment—and that does not mean showing up at someone else's wedding to see them perform. Some entertainers think nothing of inviting potential wedding clients to someone else's event—without obtaining permission—and that is the type of entertainer you do not want performing at your wedding, unless you are prepared to become the host of strangers. If a bride and groom or a social or corporate event give permission for you to drop by during set up and rehearsal, you have to be careful with how you proceed. You are setting a precedent for the request to be made to you. When your wedding set up is going on, do you want strangers around? It is better to see your chosen musician, singer, or DJ perform live at a public event.

🙠 Many musicians have CDs or taped recordings. You need to know that who you hear on the CD or tape is exactly who will be playing at your wedding (e.g., everyone who performed to create the recording will, in fact, be on stage).

Special Considerations

🙠 Think about your terms and conditions from a behavioral point of view. Do you want the musicians mingling with your guests, ordering drinks from the bar, etc.?

🙠 Find out what other additional charges will be billed back to you such as artist royalty fees (ASCAP or BMI in the United States or SOCAN in Canada), power charges, rehearsal fees, overtime charges, fees for encores, rider fees, meals, accommodation, transportation, shipping, or technical rider charges. If you are hiring a live band, make sure that they include cartage in their quote and any overtime charges that may apply. For example, if you want the instruments to remain as is and not be torn down and carted out of the room while your guests are still there, you need to be prepared to pay overtime charges for that.

🙠 Advise them of expected dress and find out if any additional charges will apply or have to be provided for them.

🙠 When choosing entertainment, you must always keep your guests in mind. Consider what is appropriate and what is not.

%a Plan on three square feet per person for the dance floor.

%a Allow twenty square feet per instrument for the musicians.

Audiovisual, Staging, and Lighting

AS YOU START to plan your wedding celebration, it will be important for you to know what the lighting in your room looks like at the time of day your ceremony and reception will take place. Will you need to bring extra lighting in or reposition the existing lighting? You will need to pay attention to where the electrical outlets are in relationship to your proposed layout—will cords or cables be visible or be in the way of your guests or waitstaff and pose potential problems? Will you be requiring extension cords? Keep in mind that power outlets are limited. Know all your electrical needs and capacity—what your caterer or facility will require for food preparation and presentation, whether you are serving blended drinks at the bar, what your music and entertainment needs are, whether you will be having an audiovisual presentation. Can all your needs be met without causing a blackout or creating a safety hazard (and does the facility keep extra fuses on hand)? You may have to bring in an electrical technician to ensure that your system will be able to handle it.

Lighting

Lighting creates mood. It adds drama to your wedding. Low lights and Candle Safe candles strategically placed can create ambience at very limited cost. Splash lights with colored gels and mirrored balls are simple and inexpensive effects. Call a lighting company that handles special events to see what can be done to enhance your wedding ceremony and reception with special effects. You may want to limit what you spend on floral arrangements and décor to do something that could possibly provide more visual impact. Lighting effects are only limited by your budget. You can opt for a full laser show as a grand finale to your wedding reception, pinspot the tables, have your room bathed in changing color, custom gobos can shine a message or your names entwined on a wall or dance floor, soft draping of the ceiling with fabric and mini lights can produce a delightful effect—many options are available to you.

What Your Audiovisual, Staging, and Lighting Company Will Need to Know

In addition to the Supplier's Information Worksheet, your supplier will need to know:

- Whether you will require audiovisual and, if so, whether it will be rear screen, front screen, or other (e.g., plasma screens)
- Whether you will require staging, what side of the room the stage will be on, and whether it will be decorated and/or draped
- Whether you will be requiring specialty lighting
- The room dimensions, including ceiling height
- What the sightlines (lines of vision) are like in the room (whether there are any pillars, hanging chandeliers, etc.)
- Whether rehearsals will be required
- Whether the facility is staffed by union employees
- What else will be taking place in the room

Questions to Ask Your Audiovisual, Staging, and Lighting Company

- Can they show you pictures or a video of the type of effects—audiovisual, staging, and lighting—they have actually done?
- Can they price their services as line items and detail their labor costs, taxes, service charges, delivery fees, etc.?
- What do they require from the sites for move-in, setup, wedding day, tear-down, and move-out?
- What other charges would you be responsible for at final billing (such as power charges, crew meals, etc.)?
- Can they price your requirements for your wedding ceremony and your wedding reception separately in case you have to make a decision based on costs to choose one or the other?

Photography

THE SAME CONSIDERATIONS apply whether or not your photographer is a professional, a family member, or a friend who takes quality photographs. You will need to look at each venue carefully and walk the facility looking though a photographer's eye. What shots and what backdrops do you want captured? How many pictures will you desire with your immediate family and wedding party members? If you start to compile a photo list, you are getting a jump on what will need to be done at some point to ensure that no pictures of specific groupings get overlooked and for your wedding photo shoot to go smoothly. In order for a photographer to price film, proofs, prints, and any applicable fees for their services, they will need to know how many photographs you will want taken and if you'll need more than one photographer to capture the pictures you want.

What Your Photographer Will Need to Know

In addition to the Supplier Information Worksheet, your photographer will need to know:

- Whether you will want photographs taken at home as you are getting ready
- Whether you will require two (or more) photographers—for example, one at your home and one at the ceremony ready to capture your arrival
- Whether posed photos will be taken at the wedding ceremony site, you will just want images captured as your wedding ceremony is unfolding, or both
- How many photographers will be required at the wedding ceremony site
- Whether you will be moving to a new location for a wedding photo shoot
- If so, what locations you are considering
- If not, whether you will be going directly to the wedding reception site
- What style of photos you will require at the wedding reception
- How long you want the photographer at the wedding reception
- How many photos you will want taken in total
- Whether you will want color or black and white photographs
- What size and quantity of prints you will require
- Whether you will want a video taken as well

Questions to Ask Your Photographer

- Where do they recommend the wedding shoot take place?
- Will you be required to obtain any permits (e.g., for photographs taken in a public park)?
- Will any site rental fees apply at the wedding shoot location?
- Will you need to reserve a time and a place for the wedding shoot location?
- Do you have any special requirements?
- How do you charge for your fees?
- What additional costs could apply, such as transportation of equipment, delivery charges, etc.?
- Will you be bringing backup batteries to ensure that we don't miss price-less shots?
- How long will it take for us to receive our contact sheets or proofs?
- Once we have selected our photos, how long will it take to receive our prints?

What to Look For

❧ Look for photographers who are experienced in taking wedding photographs and taking unposed (candid) pictures.

❧ Ask to see samples of their work.

What to Watch Out For

❧ Permits and permission may be required in advance to have your formal wedding photographs taken in a public park or private venue.

Special Considerations

❧ Advise your photographer of the expected dress code.

❧ Decide whether your photographer will be eating, drinking, and mixing with your guests.

❧ Ensure that a detailed cost list is provided, outlining exactly what you will be charged at final reconciliation. Make sure that all applicable taxes, service charges, and tipping (for assistants) is included. Have them break out the costs for each location.

Finishing Touches

WEDDING SUPPLIERS AND vendors that fall under this category are those whose costs you can assign a lump-sum dollar amount for budget purposes and whose logistical requirements are of minimal influence, pricing, or labor impact to your other wedding venue and supplier costs. These include:

❧ Wedding cake

❧ Wedding favors

❧ Bridal attire

❧ Bridal and wedding party bouquets, corsages, and boutonnieres

❧ Groom attire

❧ Wedding party attire

❧ Hairstylist

❧ Makeup

❧ Wedding rings

❧ Wedding vows

❧ Wedding official

❧ Seating chart

❧ Permits and licenses

❧ Personal shopping

❧ Wedding party gifts

❧ First night accommodations

❧ Honeymoon

Wedding Cake

&⃝ **Cost Considerations**

- Order a smaller cake for display and wedding photos and order sheet cakes made from the same ingredients to be cut and plated in the kitchen.
- Reduce the size of the wedding cake being served if you are serving a heavy dessert or setting up a sweets table.
- Will you be requiring a cake topper?

&⃝ **Critical Advance Information for Your Blueprint**

- What are the estimated costs for cake, including assembly, taxes, service charges, and delivery?
- Find out by when you will need to place your order.
- Ask how far in advance they make their wedding cakes.
- How will your wedding cake be transferred to your wedding site?
- How many wedding cakes will they be delivering and assembling on the same day?
- What assembly will be required?
- How long will assembly take?
- Who will be cutting and serving the cake? Remember to request cake plates, forks, and waitstaff to plate and serve the cake from the supplier who will be responsible for ordering your table settings.
- What time will the bakery or caterer need to access the site to assemble your wedding cake?
- What do they require from the wedding reception site (e.g., refrigeration, work table, etc.)?
- What size and shape of table (remember to order draping) will you need to provide for the cake?
- If you decide to have fresh edible flowers on your cake, who will be providing them—the bakery or the person who is handling your floral arrangements?

&⃝ **Special Considerations**

- You need to ensure that your wedding cake designer or supplier is licensed by the state health department.
- Remember your setting, the season, and your wedding cake's ingredients. For example, if your wedding will be held outdoors in the heat of summer, your wedding cake supplier needs to know that as it will affect the icing and other ingredients he or she will use.

Wedding Favors

🎀 **Critical Advance Information for Your Blueprint**

- What are the estimated costs, including assembly, taxes, service charges, and delivery?

Bridal Attire

🎀 **Critical Advance Information for Your Blueprint**

- What are the estimated budget costs, including bridal accessories?
- Find out the recommended timing of fittings so you can plot them on your Critical Path.

Tip: If you are planning an outdoor wedding ceremony or reception, one item to consider is having your wedding veil or dress weighted down so that it is not blowing all over the place during the exchange of vows or your wedding photo shoot.

Groom's Attire

🎀 **Cost Considerations**

- Do a cost comparison between renting and buying a tuxedo. If you will be attending black-tie functions in the future for business or social events, would purchasing a tuxedo be a worthwhile investment rather than a rental expense?

🎀 **Critical Advance Information for Your Blueprint**

- What are the estimated budget costs, including groom's accessories?
- Find out the recommended timing of fittings so you can plot them on your Critical Path.

Wedding Party Attire

🎀 **Critical Advance Information for Your Blueprint**

- Estimated budget costs for any wedding party attire and accessories that you will be paying for.
- Recommended timing of fittings so you can plot them on your Critical Path.

Hairstylist

🎀 **Critical Advance Information for Your Blueprint**

- What are the estimated budget costs for your and your wedding party's trial hairstyles (if applicable) you will be paying for, plus taxes and tipping?

- What are the estimated budget costs for your and your wedding party's hair that you will be paying for (plus taxes and tipping) on your wedding day?
- Find out recommended timing of trial hairstyles and your wedding day appointment so you can plot them on your Critical Path. (Make sure that there is sufficient time between your appointments and getting dressed for your wedding ceremony.)

Makeup
❧ Critical Advance Information for Your Blueprint
- What are the estimated budget costs for you and your wedding party's makeup/makeup artist trial (if applicable) that you will be paying for (plus taxes and tipping)?
- What are the estimated budget costs for you and your wedding party's makeup/makeup artist that you will be paying for (plus taxes and tipping) on your wedding day?
- Find out recommended timing of trial makeup sessions and your wedding day appointment so you can plot them on your Critical Path. (Make sure that there is sufficient time between your appointments and getting dressed for your wedding ceremony.)

Wedding Rings
❧ Critical Advance Information for Your Blueprint
- What are the estimated costs, including taxes?

Personal Shopping (Purse, Personal Care Pouch, Grooming)
❧ Critical Advance Information for Your Blueprint
- What are the estimated costs, including taxes?

Wedding Party Gifts
❧ Critical Advance Information for Your Blueprint
- What are the estimated costs, including assembly/gift wrapping, taxes, service charges, and delivery?

First Night Accommodation
❧ Critical Advance Information for Your Blueprint
- What are the estimated costs, including taxes and service charges?

Honeymoon

· What are the estimated costs, including taxes and service charges?

Get It in Writing

ONCE YOU HAVE done your initial research, spoken to potential suppliers by telephone, listened carefully to how they have handled your initial requests, perhaps done a preliminary site inspection, and narrowed down your choices of which vendors and suppliers you wish to receive a formal quote from, you will need to send them a request for a proposal in writing. This formalizes your exact requirements so that there can be no room for misunderstanding or pricing omissions by them. What you will be sending each of your selected vendors is a breakdown of your wedding day specifications with a request to receive a written quote from them.

Receiving a written quote will help you to evaluate which supplier best meets your needs. For example, you may have narrowed your selection of florists down to two or three, and seeing their proposals will allow you to see their attention to detail, their ability to make creative cost-saving recommendations, how closely they have followed your budget parameters, and areas they have overlooked that could put your wedding day event elements and budget in jeopardy. Once you have received their written quotes, it will be easy to identify their level of professionalism, their experience, and the level of service you will receive. These will be the suppliers that you will want to enter negotiation and contract talks with. You do not want to waste your time negotiating with suppliers who have proven—by the quality of the quote you have received—that they are not equipped to handle your wedding requirements.

Your request for quotes must specify exactly what you require from a specific supplier; what you need from a strategic planning, timing, logistics, and service point of view; the must-haves you want to be able to include or their creative alternatives; your list of optional enhancements you would like to have, budget permitting; and what you would need from them to move forward to contract.

What you should receive back from your vendors and suppliers is an accurate rendering of their costs and inclusions, their terms and conditions (what they will need from you and your other suppliers in order to meet your expectations), and cost saving recommendations they may have to come within your budget framework.

This process will allow you to take a step back, measure the value of your inclusions (your event elements), weigh them carefully, and make your decisions based on facts and figures without emotional attachment.

It takes time to prepare a request for a proposal, but it is time on your wedding day that you will deem well spent. You are actually moving into the planning and preparation stages of your wedding and the more you do initially, the less you have to do as your wedding date moves closer. This frees you to focus on the fun and festivities leading up to your day, knowing that all of the fine tuning has been done. What you do now and how you do it predicts the end result. Don't expect to receive more from your suppliers than you are willing to give them as they work toward building the framework of your wedding day.

It will take time to receive your quotes back from your suppliers. They will need to give thought to their pricing and the options they will be suggesting. Some will be making the time to do a quick site inspection to see your proposed venues so that they can send you their quote based on exactly what they will need to produce an extraordinary wedding day for you. You will be able to see who is taking your request seriously and putting time and effort into winning your business. Suppliers know when they receive a proposal request that it most likely will be going out to other suppliers as well and that you will be comparing costs and inclusions. They will need a minimum of two weeks to prepare their proposal for you. What some suppliers will be wary of is sharing ideas and costs and having a potential client either using their ideas and doing it on their own or revealing their ideas to other suppliers. They will be looking for assurance that that is not your intention.

A separate request for a quote is prepared for each category—not each individual supplier. For example, the Request for Proposal you would send to one floral designer would be the same as the one you would send to another floral designer or décor company you are considering to handle your floral requirements—only your cover page would change. Your formal request for a quote should include the following.

Request for Proposal Introduction and Overview

You may use the Supplier's Information Worksheet, or retype the information into a formal RFP (request for proposal). All venues and suppliers will receive the same information:

- Date you are sending the request out
- Date you will need a reply by

- The number at which they can contact you in case they require any additional information
- Whether or not you will need to conduct a preliminary site inspection

Be sure to tell each supplier that this is how you want your quote to be presented:

- Menu format with items listed as line items
- Detailed inclusions
- Breakdown of included staff
- All applicable taxes
- Service charges
- Management fees
- Permits
- Insurance
- Any additional items you will be charged for at final billing
- Delivery charges
- Electrical requirements
- Power charges
- Suggested timing
- Any special requirements for move-in, setup, wedding day orchestration, teardown, and move-out
- Items of special note, such as what they will require from other suppliers or the venue (backup generator, use of refrigerator, etc.)
- Your proposed timing of events (e.g., later afternoon wedding followed by an evening reception, dinner, and dance, or a mid-day wedding ceremony followed by a light luncheon and tea dance, etc.)
- Your wedding vision—the look and feel you want to achieve
- Your guest demographics—overview of who will be there (e.g., family and close friends, age range, descriptive makeup of group) and any traditional, cultural, religious, or protocol elements they need to be aware of (e.g., for caterers and the venue it would be essential for them to know that one of your requirements is a kosher kitchen)
- Wedding day descriptive overview, including what will be going on in each room (e.g., one-hour cocktail reception with scattered tables and chairs with open bar and passed canapés, sit-down dinner in a separate room, head table, number in wedding party, tables of eight, French-style service, bar setup in the room, dance floor, estimate of how many guests will be dancing, etc.)
- Your wedding day must-haves
- Optional enhancements you would consider if budget permits

- Your budget parameters—suppliers need this, otherwise your quote could be widely off the mark
- Your flexibility—do you want them to suggest creative cost-saving alternatives?
- Your timeline—when you will be making your decision
- To whom should they send their proposal—include all pertinent contact information (e.g., name, mailing address, telephone number, fax number, email, etc.)
- How you want to receive the proposal—hard copy, fax, email attachment, etc.?
- What format proposals should be in—Word, PDF, Excel, Lotus, or other?
- How many copies of their proposal you will require
- What you will require from them in addition to their quote (e.g., full sales kit including policies, floor plans, terms and conditions, sample contract and payment schedules, fire marshal rules and regulations, insurance requirements and required permits—all items that will aid you in making your decision as to which venue and supplier to choose)

Recommended Plan of Action

- Research venues and suppliers that fall under the "framework" category.
- Narrow down your choices, place your venues on tentative hold, and prepare and send out your written request for a quote via fax or email.
- While you are waiting for your quotes to come in, do your initial research of finishing touch wedding suppliers and cost estimates. Note: this is *not* the time to begin the actual shopping and decision-making process—that will come after you have contracted your framework suppliers and wedding sites.
- Review your responses from your proposal request and compare costs and inclusions, creative and cost-saving options, and timing and logistic requirements of each and narrow down your suppliers.
- Obtain any outstanding information and costs—as outlined by your selected suppliers.
- Begin to fill in your Wedding Day Blueprint with supplier costs and inclusions so that you know exactly where you stand from a budget perspective, areas you will need to negotiate, options, timing, and logistic items you will need to find a solution for.
- Add and subtract inclusions to see which options best fit your wedding vision and budget.
- Set up site inspection meetings with your venues and suppliers to finalize your requirements and begin contract negotiations.

Quick Overview of Possible Wedding Event Elements and Price Considerations

	Estimated Cost	Actual Cost

Venues

	Estimated Cost	Actual Cost
Site Rental		
Taxes, Service Charges, and Gratuities		
Staffing		
Gratuities		
Setup Costs		
Teardown Costs		
Cleaning		
Insurance		
Permits		

Invitations

	Estimated Cost	Actual Cost
Save the Date Cards		
Invitations		
RSVP Cards		
Thank-You Cards		
Postage		
Printing		
Calligrapher		
Custom Labels		

Transportation

	Estimated Cost	Actual Cost
Parking		
Limousines or Motor Coaches		
Parking Permits		
Valet Parking		
Traffic Direction		
Police Escort		

	Estimated Cost	Actual Cost

Wedding Ceremony Arrival

	Estimated Cost	Actual Cost
Coat Check		
Décor		
Rentals (chairs, aisle runner, etc.)		
Music and Entertainment		
Flowers		
Photographer		
Wedding Officiant		
License		

Wedding Reception

Coat Check		
Food		
Beverage		
Taxes, Service Charges, and Gratuities		
Table décor (table tops, china, crystal, silverware, linens, overlays, runners, napkins, chair covers, draping, floral arrangements, centerpieces, etc.)		
Room Décor		
Rentals (cocktail or cruiser tables, tables, chairs, etc.)		
Music and Entertainment		
Audiovisual Requirements— staging, lighting, and special effects		
Photographer		
Staffing		
Gratuities		
Print Material (place cards, menus, etc.)		
Wedding Favors		

Miscellaneous

IT IS ESSENTIAL at this stage that the only people talking to the venues and suppliers are the wedding couple. There will be a time when you can begin to hand off responsibility, but at this point you need to be in control of what is being said to venues and suppliers and hear their responses directly as it will trigger questions that need to be answered. If information is flowing in and out through multiple channels, something critical will slip through the cracks. You also need to be building a rapport with your salesperson, as you will be handling contract negotiations through them initially. You will appear disorganized and show a lack of direction if you allow anyone else to be placing calls on your behalf and flooding their sales office with messages to check this and to check that. You can bring others in, selectively, under your specific instruction, but there is less room for error and misunderstanding if all information goes through one central person—be it the bride, the groom, or someone elected to handle the majority of the planning.

If you want to pull off a polished and professional wedding, you must present a polished, professional, and pulled-together front going in. While it is still best to manage things yourself, you can enlist others' help by having someone organize the quotes that will be arriving from your venues and suppliers.

It is important to read all the information that arrives as every supplier presents its information differently and you can pick up key points from their proposals. You will be able to identify areas some suppliers have missed or glossed over when, in fact, the areas they are not addressing in detail could affect your budget, timing, or logistics, as well as hidden costs that may be transparent on another supplier's quote. This is not an area that you can hand off, as you need to absorb all the information and the facts in order to make sound choices. Highlight or make notes in the margins of important data that you will need to refer back to when you go to enter it on your Wedding Blueprint breakdown. Be careful not to use a highlighter on any fax paper that is marker-sensitive as once you have highlighted over it, you will not be able to read it.

As you are working on one specific area of your wedding planning, you need easy access to the rest of your files—what your food and beverage supplier may be noting may be something you will need to question your décor company about. Once everything is in place from a contract standpoint, you can then get rid of excess material from suppliers you will not be using. Call them to thank them for their information and let them know that you have decided to go with another company.

There will be a point (Step 7), when you can begin to bring in others to help you in your wedding day orchestration. At Step 8, you will begin handling over responsibility. At Step 9, you will let go of responsibility entirely, so that you can focus only on what you need to do at that point.

Staying Centered About Finances

What to Ask Before You Sign on the Dotted Line

YOUR QUOTES ARE in; you've narrowed down your choices for your wedding ceremony, reception venues, and suppliers; and plugged all your estimated costs into your Wedding Day Blueprint. You are now in a position to know your opinions and make informed decisions regarding your next two steps—final contract negotiations and signing your letters of agreement with your venues and suppliers.

Your contract negotiations will be based on two important elements—pricing and contractual terms and conditions. You may very well need concessions and creative options on both before you can commit to your guest count and which event elements you will be including.

You may have found when you sat down and began to carefully review your proposed costs and must-have wedding day inclusions that your guest list exceeds the number of dollars you have to spend. Does this mean that you then sit down and begin to pare down your list of invited guests? No. This is the time you sit down and begin to compare the different ways your dollars can be spent. This is where your suppliers' creativity comes into play.

What you can't do is simply adjust the number of guests or delete main components and still use the figures you have been quoted. Your proposals have been based on a specific number of guests and the revenue your suppliers will be making, which was based on the inclusions you outlined in your request. If your guest count goes up or down and major elements are added and subtracted, your suppliers will need to tender a new price quote to you.

What you can do is look at your wedding must-haves and prioritize them. It is possible to plan and execute an exquisite stand-up reception for one hundred guests that is just as beautiful and meaningful as a sit-down cocktail reception and dinner for fifty. It is up to you to decide which matters most—having a larger gathering and including more of those you love or a smaller, more intimate, but inclusive affair. Neither is right or wrong, but you will be required to choose.

If, for instance, the group of one hundred includes people you are not really close to, see only in business, and some you don't even know, the decision to have a more intimate affair in the manner you envisioned first could be easy. If they are all dear to you and limiting your guest list would sit uneasily on you today, it could become a wedding regret if you hold dinner as being the more important must-have of the two. At this point, you need to trust your inner feelings and turn to your suppliers for creative possibilities. You may have discovered when you reexamined your guest list that seventy-five is the number that matters most to you.

Now your suppliers have the opportunity to shine by showing you how your costs can be brought into line. What you didn't have when you started the process is all the costs and all of the facts. You do now. This will enable you to hear clearly and understand what your suppliers are trying to convey when you go back to them and say that the dinner menu must come in at a specific dollar amount to remain at the same guest count. Then ask what must be done to come in at that figure. Repeat this process with all of your event elements.

Menus can be scaled up or down and custom created. Lobster ravioli may be suggested as an alternative to a more expensive lobster appetizer you were hoping to include. Both can be plated and presented elegantly, but there can be big cost savings. Expensive cuts of meats can become half portions with another less costly—but complementary—half portion. Drinks can be poured at one ounce instead of one-and-a-half ounces per drink. You can change your bar from premium brands to standard. Serve house wines as opposed to more expensive vintages.

Bring down the cost of desserts by doing something fun or eye catching instead of wildly expensive, especially if you are serving wedding cake immediately or soon after. Start thinking presentation. Desserts can be festive without being excessive. An ice cream sundae bar can be set up for guests to serve themselves. This food station display serves a dual purpose. After a sit-down dinner, you are providing your guests with a reason to stand and move about the room and greet other guests as they compare their ice cream creations. Ice cream sundaes are not just for kids—one airline serves them to businesspeople in first class and they are one of their most requested desserts.

Areas of creative compromise can bring your costs down considerably without compromising the integrity of your wedding vision or budget. Once you have your costs and inclusions aligned with your budget, you will be able to move ahead to contracting.

It is critical that your contract captures everything that has been agreed upon. This includes any special concessions made during negotiations and general discussions right up to the time of signing. What is of extreme importance as you move into the final negotiations and contract stage is to remember that the person you are dealing with today most likely will *not* be the one you will be working with once the contract is signed. In most instances, you will have started your wedding planning with a venue or supplier sales representative.

Once your wedding is contracted and sold, it then moves into their operations department. You will be given a new contact to work with. They will be involved in fine tuning your details, your timing, and logistical requirements. Their point of reference will be "the contract." They will be continually pulling you back to the terms and conditions you agreed to. It is essential that you take the time to review your contracts thoroughly and cross-check them against your request for a quote, their proposal, and your wedding blueprint. Doing this can save you hours of frustration later on if an event element has been overlooked.

You cannot depend on going back to your salesperson. They will have moved on in terms of planning the next wedding and unless you have written proof that an item was negotiated or a concession was made, they may not remember whether it was or not. Their first step will be referring to the signed contact and shifting through their notes. The responsibility is on you to make sure that what was discussed appears in your contract.

You cannot take someone's verbal okay that everything has been looked after. Initial items that are being contracted, changes, concessions, and amendments must all be documented and signed off on by both parties to be legally binding. It is imperative that you receive written quotes and go over your contracts with a fine-toothed comb. You cannot afford not to because it does not stop with the transfer from sales to wedding operations. The person handling your on-site wedding arrangements could be someone entirely new as your file is passed forward again to a new department that oversees the actual wedding day. Once again, they will be operating from your signed contact and if there are no authorized amendments made, that is exactly what will be showing up on your wedding day. Ways to prevent something from slipping through the cracks every time your file changes hands are outlined in upcoming chapters. However, you must begin with a strong foundation—your signed contract.

Cost and Contract Negotiations

NEGOTIATIONS WILL BE going on with your suppliers until you near your wedding date. Negotiations are skillfully done in layers. At this step, it is important to undertake the major items and have them in place so that you know exactly where you stand. Right now your focus is on cost concession, to bring your budget in line, and contract compromises on red-flag areas as you begin to unveil hidden costs and concerns. As you enter into your contract negotiations, there are three main points to keep in mind.

1. If you are looking to a supplier to bring down costs, you need to look for items where there is room either to maneuver the price downward or to have a cost waived. A supplier who is providing just one item (e.g., wedding favors) and who may only have a small profit margin to begin with, will not be in a position to make concessions. You don't want to nickel and dime a supplier to death because it could backfire on your wedding day, costing you in quality or service. You have to create a means where your suppliers are still making a profit but you are meeting your needs. They do have a business to run and if they are not profitable, they will soon be out of business.

   Your food and beverage suppliers and venues are selling the bigger ticket items. The margin on bar beverages is usually a much larger profit margin than a floral centerpiece, for example. Your beverage supplier may be able to waive or reduce add-on costs for garnishes, bartender charges, or replenishing fees. Your food provider should be able to custom create a menu that will fit into your budget or provide you with a flat rate to serve unlimited canapés for a set period of time instead of charging you per item. If you are holding your wedding reception in a hotel and having food and beverages, room rental charges while your event is taking place will most likely be waived. You may be charged a room rental fee if your setup requires they miss earning revenue from a breakfast or a lunch, but these charges can be reduced. With suppliers for rental items, the hard costs are labor and transportation—the chairs, tables, linens, etc., have been paid for many times over. If they can't reduce the rental amount, they may be open to upgrading your choices at no additional charge.

2. You must negotiate with someone who can authorize a concession. If you do not receive the response you require and it is a fair request, you must be prepared to ask to speak with someone more senior and make your decisions

having fully explored your options. Your request to go higher should be handled with tact and finesse. Your intention is not to alienate your sales representative—they may simply not be in position to give you a "yes."

3. Put your cards on the table and be prepared to walk away if the terms and conditions are not right for you.

As you read through your contracts, mark any potential red-flag areas you come across. It is essential that you understand fully what they can mean to you from a financial and legal standpoint. Review each and every clause carefully. Following are some pitfalls to watch out for.

Event Cancellation

Some facilities charge not only the deposit and fees they have collected up to the point of cancellation, they also try to recoup their losses and damages by collecting the outstanding fees listed in the proposal that could be billed under "genuine and reasonable pre-estimate of the losses and damages" they are now suffering if you decide to cancel or move your dates. This is not money for staffing and other inclusions, which are dollars they will not be spending if your event is cancelled. This is the money they would have earned—their profit—had the event taken place. Requesting that the specific dollar amount be detailed in the contract would be recommended as opposed to leaving it open-ended for future interpretation. For example, many venue contracts will detail the dates and the cancellation dollar amounts that include their "losses and damages" with their loss and damage amounts escalating the closer to the event date you go.

Cancellation Date	Cancellation Penalty
Upon Signing	$
Twelve Months Prior to Your Wedding	$$
Eight Months Prior to Your Wedding	$$$
Six Months Prior to Your Wedding	$$$$
Three Months Prior to and Up to and Including Your Wedding Date	$$$$$

Their applicable cancellation dates and dollar amounts are spelled out. You know exactly what you are liable for if you need to cancel or change your wedding date. There should be no reason that the dollar amount cannot be calculated and laid out.

Others may charge their full loss and damages immediately upon signing your contract or at specified date.

Cancellation Date	Cancellation Penalty
Upon Signing	$
Twelve Months Prior to and Up to and Including Your Wedding Date	$$$$$

You need to know exactly what you are facing. From there you can begin negotiating. For example, some properties will refund cancellation penalties if they resell the space. Some offer it up front as part of their terms and conditions. Others will review it if it is brought forward to them as part of your terms and conditions of signing, and will concede. They lose nothing if it is rented out and the same dollar value is realized and, if it is not resold, they still are protected. To use a cliché, it is "win-win" for both of you. They are demonstrating a spirit of give and take, not just take. They may also allow you to change your date without paying the full penalty. You will never know what can be done if you do not ask.

Companies that refuse to even entertain your request are setting themselves up to earn twice the room revenue they would have received. Their contracts are one-sided and you have to decide if this is a company you want to do business with. If you find yourself up against this scenario where you are paying the same fees that you would be if you were still using the room, ask if that means it is still yours to do with what you choose (if you cancel all the other elements—even if it means it sits empty—as they would already have been compensated in full). Their response will be very telling. It could mean that they revisit their policy and make a concession and, if not, you know exactly where you stand before you sign on the dotted line.

Payment Schedule

Watch for language like this in your contract: "Supplier must be in receipt of both the signed contract and first deposit in order to secure the date, services, and function space requested. If the second and third deposits, as set out above, have not been received by the required date, the room booking and services will be considered tentative and may be forfeited to any second or third holds without notice."

The signed contract and first deposit are not a concern. You would not be signing the contract if you were not prepared to put down your deposit. What it is important to note, track, and plan for is your second and third deposits. If you need to move the payment due dates to match your paydays, the time to do so is at contracting, not after the contract has been signed. Take the time to look at where you will be financially and if the payment dates will cause any difficulties. Do you need to move them a couple of days, a couple of weeks, or even by a month? What they are telling you is that if you miss those payment dates, your booking may be forfeited to any second or third holds without notice.

Venues are prepared to act swiftly if they have to. Their product is space and time and they cannot make up for their losses if a date goes unsold. Their product is time sensitive and, as such, creates a sense of urgency. It is also important to note that they are telling their clients up front that they will be taking second and third holds on your space—they will have people waiting in the wings to step in and take over your wedding venue, date, and time (something to keep in mind should you find your preferred venue already booked). Also watch out if the contract gives the supplier the right to charge interest for the number of days of late payment. Being late with your payments can then be a costly error.

Guest Guarantee

Watch for language such as: "The Client agrees to provide a final guarantee of the number of guests by 12:00 noon at least five business days prior to the scheduled date of the Event. The Client acknowledges and agrees that if he or she fails to provide such written notification, the Client will be responsible to pay the full costs applicable to the number of guests identified in this contract."

The date they are giving you is the date and time for your final food and beverage guarantees. What needs to be noted is that it is has to be received in writing (not called in), it must be received at least five *business* days (not at least five days) before your event, and it must be received by 12:00 noon. Missing the term "business days" or the cut-off time is a common error that can leave couples scrambling. They may find that their deadline passed and they are now contractually liable for paying for their original guest count. It is important to add this key date and time to your critical path, which will be discussed in Step 7. Ask your venue to write the actual date into your contract so there is no misunderstanding.

They are putting the responsibility on you to remember; they will not be calling you to remind you that it is due.

You may also encounter this: "Should the final guest count decrease by 20 percent or more of the original booking, a surcharge for loss of revenue may be applied or Supplier reserves the right to assign the Event a different function space or implement a surcharge for loss of revenue."

Should your numbers drop more than 20 percent, the venue will have the right to move your event out of the room that you have selected and built your wedding around. If you want to stay in that room, you may have to pay a fee to do so. Going into your contract, you need to carefully consider your guest count. It can affect you financially in the end. What would also need clarification is if whether or not you can drop your guest count by 19 percent without any penalty.

Check with the facility before giving your initial guest count to see if they build an "overage" into their quotes. This applies whether you are doing your food through a venue or a caterer. What some facilities do is prepare 5 percent or 10 percent more than the food guarantee in case there are last-minute guests. You might be able to use this to your financial advantage. For example, if you are expecting a guest count of one hundred guests, and the venue does calculate overage into their figures, they will have food on hand for one hundred five guests (based on 5 percent overage). You could reduce your food and beverage guarantee to ninety-six guests (check with your venue) as opposed to one hundred. If you have any last minute cancellations due to illness, etc. (up to four), you may save the cost of their meal. If everyone does show up, you will have food and beverage on hand for one hundred and will be charged on one hundred guests attending. What you have to find out from the venue is how this will affect your table settings. Will they still set for one hundred guests, even though your guarantee is for ninety-six, and only charge you for the number of guests served over ninety-six?

Preferred Caterers and Suppliers Clauses

If your venue is not providing the food and beverages, you may encounter something like this: "Catering services are provided by a preferred list of qualified caterers, who rank among the finest in the area. No other caterer shall be permitted within the premises without the prior written consent and approval of Venue, which consent can be unreasonably or arbitrarily withheld. A commission fee of 15 percent on the cost of the food, based on the market value of said food, will be added to the final invoice for all caterers. The Client may not prepare or bring in their own food."

What is essential to note is that the venue is charging 15 percent on the cost of food the caterer is bringing in as a commission. Not only are you paying for the food, the taxes, service charges, and gratuities, you now have to factor in a 15 percent commission fee to the venue, as well as a management fee to the caterer. Your $2.00 per appetizer could come in at close to $4.00 apiece. Multiply that by the number of pieces and number of guests and your food and beverage costs could increase by hundreds if not thousands of dollars more than expected. This is something that could easily be overlooked. For you to be able to make your decisions based on actual costs, it must be added into your Wedding Day Blueprint. What you may find is that it may not be listed in your caterer's quote under "not included," as it is a term and condition of the venue's contract, not theirs. Caterers who do make note of this fact on their quote are watching out for your dollars and trying to keep you informed. If two caterers have submitted bids to you, where one mentions it and the other does not, it does not mean that it does not have to be paid. When choosing any supplier, you can't make your decision based on price alone. Attention to detail is extremely important and should be part of your decision-making process.

This example demonstrates why it is so important to have all venue and supplier contracts or a boilerplate sample, as well as any general policies before you start to contract—otherwise you are placing yourself in a catch-22 position. Again, you are working with a domino effect as each venue and supplier can affect another logistically and financially. If this condition places the venue out of your reach, you need to be able to go to them before you contract to see if the 15 percent commission can be waived entirely or reduced substantially. Talk to your caterer to see how costs can be brought down. You will also need to know if the 15 percent commission will be levied on any beverages your caterer is handling.

Service Staff Clauses

Watch for this clause in regards to the staff: "To maintain the service standards of Supplier, all service staff, including but not limited to: waiters, bartenders, hosts, coat check, security, and ushers, will be provided by Supplier and billed to the Client based on actual hours worked, with a four hour minimum booking per staff member being applicable. In addition, Supplier reserves the right to set the number of staff required for an Event to ensure appropriate staff to guest ratios to maintain service excellence."

The venue is letting you know that they have the right to determine the number of staff required to be brought in and that the charge for their services will be based on a minimum of four hours each. What you will need to know up front is the number of staff; the number of estimated hours; if there are any applicable taxes, service charges, and gratuities charged on these amounts; and if and when overtime hours kick in. You will also need to find out if there are mandatory meals that you will have to include to feed any of the staff members. You can negotiate to see if there are any areas or fees that that can be waived to help bring your costs down.

Coat Check Clauses

A coat check clause might read: "Supplier will operate a coat check within the facility. Host coat check will be $2.50 per item checked, based on final confirmed guest count. Coat check will be mandatory from October to April. For a cash coat check, the charge will be $1.75 per item. Minimum coat check items will be required for a cash coat check format."

Not only are you being charged for coat check staff as per the previous contract clause, but if you were to delve further, you will also find listed in this clause that they do make coat check mandatory at specific times of the year and you will be billed per item checked. This again is another cost you will need to capture on your Wedding Day Blueprint. Once again, find out if taxes, service charges, and gratuities will be charged in addition to this amount at final reconciliation. You could approach the facility regarding waiving all these charges.

Delivery Clauses

Language for delivery clauses might read: "Items such as flowers, decorations, gifts, brochures, etc., are to be delivered only on the Event day and at least three hours before the function. Notice of delivery must be made to the Event Coordinator in order to secure proper loading dock placement. Deliveries outside normal business hours must be approved by Venue in advance and deliveries sent before the scheduled day of the Event may be subject to a storage fee. Venue will not assume any responsibility for items delivered."

Suppliers will need to know their delivery cut-off dates and that the schedule must be adhered to as they will need to block space. The facility is also saying they may charge you a storage fee for deliveries received in advance of your wedding day. You will need to find out when these will apply and how much the charges are. You will also need to check if any other fees will be incurred (e.g., loading dock and use of their equipment). You will need to let your suppliers know that the facility is taking no responsibility for the delivered goods. Depending on what is being delivered, adding security could be something that you will need to add to your budget. Delivery is often an area where special concessions can be made and charges dropped, but you will need to negotiate this before contracting.

Insurance and Protection of Property Clauses

Here are a couple of examples of insurance and protection of property clauses. Watch out for language such as: "The Client shall provide to Venue at least ten business days prior to the Event, a certificate of Commercial General Liability insurance issued by an Insurance company acceptable to Venue to cover the Event. Commercial General Liability insurance shall provide a minimum liability of $2,000,000 for bodily injury, personal injury, and/or property damage in any one occurrence and shall include a cross-liability clause, naming Venue as an additional insured, and shall provide that the Policy will not be terminated once issued, unless Venue is given thirty days' written notice of such cancellation by registered mail. The Policy shall also contain a waiver of rights of subrogation, which the insurer may have against Venue and those for whom Venue is responsible whether or not the damage or injury is caused by any omission or negligence of Venue or such persons to whom in law it is responsible."

"The Client shall be responsible for loss or damage done to Venue due to negligence, theft, or abuse on the part of the Client's guests, employees, contractors, servants, or anyone else invited or contracted by the Client. The Client acknowledges that Venue assumes no responsibility for Client's equipment and property at the facility from occurrences including, without limitation, fire, theft, and vandalism and that protection as such is the responsibility of the Client. The Client will also ensure any contractors hired by the Client are aware of the Event and the Rules and Regulations of Venue and Venue will assume no responsibility unless caused by Venue's willful misconduct or negligence."

Go through your contract's clauses dealing with insurance and protection of property carefully. If the venue does not receive what it needs, when it needs it, they can refuse to let your suppliers start moving in. It is crucial that you are on top of your venue and supplier insurance requirements. The same can apply if you or your suppliers have not obtained applicable permits (e.g., liquor license).

You can and will be charged with damages. If you have a case of "guests gone wild," it can be expensive.

Each of your venue and supplier contracts may refer to their standard rules and regulations, but not list them in the body of their contract. It will be up to you to make sure that you receive a copy, carefully review the content, and advise your other suppliers of anything they need to be aware of. These are generally not in their brochure as that is a sales piece, but are detailed in a separate pamphlet or handout that you could easily overlook that is generally included when requesting a full sales kit. They may be itemized or listed throughout the material in the fine print. You need to incorporate due diligence and critical costs and items into your Wedding Day Blueprint before you contract with any of your suppliers.

Agreement of Terms

Somewhere in every contract you will be signing, you will be advised that you are agreeing to the terms laid out in the contract and the fact that both parties must approve any changes or amendments in writing. You will have been served notice that verbal okays to costs and concessions will be meaningless. To protect yourself, your contract must clearly define all terms and conditions you are agreeing to from the very beginning. Do not hesitate to ask any of your venues or suppliers to prepare a revised contract or a written amendment. Never sign a contract until the changes you have requested have been made.

After you have reviewed all your contracts and read the fine print in each and every policy, all the general information, and the terms and conditions that will apply, you are in a position to sign off on them. You cannot afford to overlook the clauses outlined in your contracts. You have to enter this step aware of all that is entailed in maximizing all your options. Many of the clauses listed in this section can be waived, reduced, amended, or adjusted if you make them part of your contract negotiations. Most importantly, once you have received concessions on various items, have the changes and amendments clearly spelled out in your contract and properly signed off on by someone who is an authorized signing officer of the company. Once you have signed the contract, you will have lost your negotiating advantage and be legally bound to their terms and conditions.

Finalize—Not Sign—Your Contracts Checklist

Before you sign your contracts, you must go over all of the details very carefully. Review each of the following details of the contracts.

- Written quote laid out in menu format with all applicable taxes, service charges, and tipping (and how they are calculated), plus any other charges that will be billed at final reconciliation.
- Sample contract to review.
- Sample payment schedule to review.

- Attrition dates (dates you can reduce quantities, guest numbers, and food and beverage guarantees without penalty).
- Number guarantee dates.
- Cancellation charges.
- Terms and conditions.
- Policies.
- General information and general catering information.
- Electrical requirements.
- Required permits to obtain (e.g., liquor licenses, host and supplier liability insurance) and who is responsible for them.
- Legal room capacity.
- Fire marshal rulings to be aware of and required permits.
- What is going on before your wedding, after your wedding, and during your wedding with regards to move-in, setup, actual events, teardown, and move-out, and how it could affect your wedding (e.g., noise, block access for move-in, etc.).
- Find out from your suppliers if they are handling only your event that day or rushing to or from another event which could put yours in any jeopardy.

Planning for Ease

Creating Your Critical Path

THE GOOD NEWS is that you are now in the home stretch. The research and development that you already put into your design and planning stages will help you fly through the final stages. The work you have already done will now allow you to relax before your big day and really enjoy being with each other, your family, friends, and guests before you enter this new chapter of your life.

Right now, having followed the planning principles in this book, you know exactly what your finalized wedding vision looks like, what needs to be done, how it should be done, when it needs to be done, why it must be done, and exactly how much it is all going to cost. You know when and where you need to pull back and are continually on the lookout for creative cost-saving ideas and areas of negotiation. You know what resonates with your wedding vision—feels right, feels good, and defines you as a couple—and you are able to focus on what needs to be done next, which is preparing your Critical Path.

Your Critical Path is going to turn your wedding day vision into your wedding day reality. Your critical path is a master "to do" list where you will begin to plot the timelines, delivery schedules, confirmation dates, and supplier and venue requirements that you and your wedding team need to be on top of. You will see clearly what has to be done and by when; where you will have personal, professional, and wedding planning crunch periods; and on which tasks you can begin to bring others in. You already have the majority of information you need, outlined in your various contracts, correspondence, and Wedding Blueprint breakdown.

You can set up your Critical Path manually or on your computer. Using your computer is more efficient because it is easier to add and subtract items in sequential order and print out revised copies for everyone involved. In order to begin to prepare your critical path, you will need:

- A blank calendar. (The calendar in this planner is set up so the week begins on Monday, not Sunday. It will be helpful to see the weekend as a block of time in which to focus on wedding plans.)
- A set of colored highlighters
- Pencils with good erasers
- All your supplier contracts
- All your correspondence from your selected venues and suppliers
- Your revised Wedding Vision Overview grid and outline
- Your revised Wedding Day Blueprint

This is the time when you will also be sorting through your signed contracts and quotes and pulling essential material to file in your planner.

Charting Your Critical Path

- Begin your Critical Path by laying out the number of months from contracting to your actual wedding date as headings. For the last two months before your wedding, begin to break it down into weeks. Make note of contract business day cutoff dates at the top so they will continue to stand out in your mind and be easily identifiable. Remember it is business days prior to your supplier contract fulfillment begins, which is not necessarily your wedding date. (If your décor company's setup begins a day or more prior to your wedding date, that is their start date. The same would apply for your venue as they would be contracted to allow an early move in.) You are calculating for contract guarantee cutoff dates, not the actual number of days prior, and conceivably you will have different business cutoff dates for various suppliers. List them in sequential order as well.
- Under the applicable month, fill in all major holidays where offices will be closed and you will be unable to reach people.
- Add in known times when you and your intended will be unavailable due to business or personal travel. Put these and all the following dates in sequential order.

✤ Note professional or personal time crunches when your workload is heavy (e.g., year-end at work, company office moving, exams, preparing for graduation, competitions, etc.).

✤ Find out and mark down when key people in your family and wedding party will be away for business or pleasure.

✤ Check to see if any of your main wedding venue and supplier contacts know when they will be away from the office.

✤ From your contracts, list your payment dates, attrition dates, food and beverage guarantee dates, and other guarantee dates.

✤ From all your suppliers' policies, terms, and conditions, list any cutoff dates that could affect your wedding and your wedding suppliers.

✤ Record all dates when you must receive copies of permits and insurance from your suppliers.

✤ List all dates that copies of all permits and insurance paperwork must be submitted to your venue or fire marshal.

✤ From your supplier quotes and Wedding Day Blueprint, start listing applicable time lines (e.g., when copy for wedding invitations will need to be in, first proof date of invitation, song list to musicians, date the photographer requires the master wedding photo shoot list, etc.). Remember to keep listing all entries in sequential order.

✤ Fill in dates for cutoff that you are aware of (e.g., when invitations for guest list A will need to be mailed, RSVP date for guest list A, when guest list B invitations will go out, seating chart to be finalized, etc.).

✤ Add in all known personal events, such as engagement parties, bridal showers, bachelor and bachelotte parties, bridal fittings, makeup rehearsal, tux fitting, family events, celebrations, time for holiday shopping, nights when you have scheduled activities, hair appointment for your wedding day, etc.

✤ List all supplier site inspection dates and scheduled meetings.

✤ Schedule in times for budget updates—this can be daily or weekly as prices are finalized.

🌿 Wedding Critical Path Worksheet

Month:_____ Begin wedding planning

- _____
- _____
- _____

Month:_____

- _____
- _____
- _____

Month:_____

- _____
- _____
- _____

Month:_____

- _____
- _____
- _____

Month:_____

- _____
- _____
- _____

Month:_____ Twelve weeks prior to our wedding

- _____
- _____
- _____

60 business days prior guarantee (date/supplier)

- _____
- _____
- _____

Wedding Critical Path Worksheet (cont.)

Month:_____ Eight weeks prior to our wedding

- _____
- _____
- _____

45 business days prior guarantee (date/supplier)

- _____
- _____
- _____

Month:_____ Six weeks prior to our wedding

- _____
- _____
- _____

30 business days prior guarantee (date/supplier)

- _____
- _____
- _____

Month:_____ Four weeks prior to our wedding

- _____
- _____
- _____

21 business days prior guarantee date (date/supplier)

- _____
- _____
- _____

Three weeks prior to our wedding—14 business days prior guarantee (date/supplier)

- _____
- _____
- _____

Two weeks prior to our wedding—5 business days prior guarantee (date/supplier)

- _____
- _____
- _____

One week prior to our wedding

- _____
- _____
- _____

Six days prior to our wedding

- _____
- _____
- _____

Five days prior to our wedding

- _____
- _____
- _____

Four days prior to our wedding

- _____
- _____
- _____

Three days prior to our wedding

- _____
- _____
- _____

Two days prior to our wedding

- _____
- _____
- _____

One day prior to our wedding—Wedding Rehearsal Morning

- _____
- _____
- _____
- _____
- _____

One day prior to our wedding—Wedding Rehearsal Afternoon

- _____
- _____
- _____
- _____
- _____

One day prior to our wedding—Wedding Rehearsal Evening

- _____
- _____
- _____
- _____
- _____

Wedding Day—Morning

- _____
- _____
- _____
- _____
- _____

Wedding Day—Afternoon

- _____
- _____
- _____
- _____
- _____

Wedding Day—Two hours prior

- _____
- _____
- _____
- _____
- _____
- _____
- _____

Wedding Day—One hour prior

- _____
- _____
- _____
- _____
- _____
- _____
- _____

Wedding Ceremony

- _____
- _____
- _____
- _____
- _____
- _____
- _____

Wedding Reception

- _____
- _____
- _____
- _____
- _____
- _____
- _____

Once everything is laid out in month and date order, it is easy to see where you will be facing wedding overload and where your personal and business timelines will be colliding with deadlines. What you have before you at this moment is only your Critical Path guideline. Now you must begin to schedule your Critical Path backwards and build in time buffers and move deadlines around to allow you to have breathing space. But before you do so, transfer all actual contractual and critical deadlines to your calendar as a reminder backup.

When it is filled out in entirety, you can pass it over to a family member or friend who is organized and who is prepared to act as head of your advance team on your wedding day. They can work in conjunction with your family members, maid or matron of honor, and best man up until your wedding, but on your actual wedding day, they will be the one overseeing your on-site wedding orchestration and will be your suppliers' main contact. Your family and attendants' attention will be on you that day, not on the suppliers, musicians, photographers, staff, etc. If you do not have someone who can act in that capacity for you on your wedding day, you may want to look at professional freelance event directors or wedding planning help you can hire. Your suppliers will be able to give you contact names.

These dates must remain listed in order on your Critical Path so that you always are aware of them and have them handy if you need to do some additional juggling down the road. Leave them as they are on your Critical Path, but on your calendar, back up their due date by three or more days—pick a day of the week that is appropriate, fits in with your schedule, is not a holiday—and enter your deadlines in sequential order. You have to give yourself leeway (e.g., do not schedule to call in your food and beverage guarantee on the same day as your expected RSVPs come in, as you will need time to figure out whether the final count will also affect your options before faxing or emailing in your final numbers). Building in buffers is essential.

Pay careful attention to the last month before your wedding. Your goal is to clear as much from that month as possible and move items that you can to an earlier due date. Have the last two weeks entirely clear of outstanding wedding planning issues—there is no need to be planning right down to the wire. For example, your musicians may need your song list one month before your wedding, but if you can give it to them two or three months earlier than they require it, you are freeing yourself up to do other things. You want to get as much as possible out of the way as early as you can so that you can finalize your Wedding Flow sheets, but you must be realistic. By laying out all your upcoming commitments and deadlines—personal, professional, and wedding planning—in month and date order, you know early on what is in front of you. If your Critical Path shows that your year-end at work is coming exactly at the time you need to be verifying the correct spelling of names and addresses for your guest list, you know that you have to move that up and ask for help in this area. That is a task where you can bring others in and can begin as soon as you compile your proposed guest lists. The invitations can be sitting, stuffed, sealed, and waiting to be mailed if you have a specific date you want to mail them on.

Professional event and wedding planners do as much as they can immediately upon contracting. They will continue to touch base with their suppliers on a regular basis, checking in to see if anything needs to be updated and calling in numbers when needed, but the bulk of the work is done early on and they are on to the next project. That is what you need to work toward. Having as much done as possible early on allows you to relax and take your time finding the perfect wedding dress, having a wedding makeup and hair rehearsal with your friends, taking dance lessons to prepare for your first dance together, shopping for wedding rings, writing your wedding vows, meeting with family and friends, and planning your life together.

Your Critical Path will remain fluid as new items are added and you finalize timing and logistics with your suppliers. Remember to cross off or mark in some way (e.g., highlight, not delete), what has been done on your Critical Path. It will serve as a reminder that it has been looked after and what remains to be done will stand out and draw your attention to it. If you make changes, date them and create a revised Critical Path, otherwise it will be confusing. If it is just one item here or there and you have captured as much as possible up front, you can add them in pencil. Keep old copies for reference, but you may want to move them out of your planner into a separate "dead information" file and keep only what you are currently working on in your wedding planner.

Once you have signed your contracts, updated your Wedding Day Blueprint, revised your Wedding Flow sheets, prepared your Critical Path, reviewed your dates, built in time buffers, and moved as much as possible out of your final month of planning, you will find that you are in total control of your wedding elements, know them inside-out, and are knowledgeable about all the terms and conditions you have to meet. Building in your personal and professional (work) commitments allows you to see in advance the problem areas that could leave you frazzled if you do not take action to diffuse them by pulling in help and moving due dates to a better (earlier) timeframe. This also allows you to prepare your family members and wedding party by giving them advance notice of when, where, and how you will need their help so that they can make any necessary adjustments to their personal and work schedules to be there for you.

The earlier you can finalize details with your suppliers, the better it is for them as well. They are juggling a number of special events and weddings and the more organized you are, the better they will be able to service you and help you create the wedding of your dreams.

As mentioned earlier, the burden is fully on you for meeting payment dates and calling in guarantees. Do not look to your suppliers to call you and remind you that a deadline is approaching. That seldom occurs and their contract waives them of any obligation to do so. It will be your responsibility to be on top of your timelines, guarantees, and commitments—which is easy to do once your Critical Path is in place. The time and effort you put into designing your Critical Path will be well spent and it will prove to be of great value to you in the end.

Go with the Flow

Flow Sheets Make Your Wedding Day
Flawless and Relaxed

WEDDING FLOW SHEETS serve many purposes. First and foremost they are a written outline of your requirements. They are laid out in chronological order and detail your requirements, inclusions, costs, standards, and expectations. They lessen the margin for error and misunderstanding and become the operating manual from which your wedding day vision is orchestrated. For example, if you have a sweets table, coffee, and tea service slated for the end of the night, you may be looking for a more gracious layout than your facility may be planning. They may be approaching it from a service and staffing standpoint while you are looking at it through your guests' eyes. For them, it may be standard practice simply to bring out stacks of cups and stacks of saucers and simply place them side by side and teaspoons thrown together in an upright container. It is easy and fast to do. For your guests' convenience and a more pleasing setup, having the cup placed on the saucer with a teaspoon on the side and displaying them in this manner is preferable. It is easier for your guests to pick up in one smooth motion as they may also be balancing a dessert cake and fork. Setting them out in this manner, however, is more labor intensive for the staff and, if you do not mention it as a preference, it will not be done. The same applies for something as simple as milk, cream, and sugar. Your vision may have been raw sugar cubes and tongs and fresh milk and cream in silver serving vessels, while their normal display is sugar packets and disposable creamer containers, plastic stir sticks with a waste basket that quickly becomes unsightly. A wedding requires more finesse. There is generally no additional cost to provide upgraded service and amenities, but it is a matter of clearly laying out your expectations at the very beginning as they apply to timing, setup, service, and style.

Your Wedding Flow sheets also serve three other very important functions all equally important to a smooth and stress-free wedding day delivery. First, once you have compiled them in date and time order for your venue and various suppliers, you will have created a master operations plan. Copies of your Wedding Flow sheets can then be dispatched to all parties involved. While your wedding favor company, for example, will only require what is pertinent to them, your venue, caterer, décor company, entertainment management company, florist, rental company, and other major suppliers will benefit by knowing exactly what else will be happening; how it will be happening; and when during move in, setup, wedding day, teardown, and move out. They will be able to advise you immediately of any problem areas so that you can take immediate action now to circumvent them. If there are any areas of concern or contention as to what is and is not included, you are dealing with them well in advance of your wedding day. Wedding Flow sheets eliminate surprises, unexpected costs, and any event element being overlooked.

The second advantage your Wedding Flow sheets will provide is that they take you through your wedding setup day by day, minute by minute. You can see exactly where you need to assign areas of responsibility to specific members of your family, wedding party, and friends who have volunteered their services to help out on your wedding day and the days leading up to it. You will need people on hand to oversee deliveries, ensure that what has been ordered does arrive and is as ordered—one couple found their wedding favors tied with ribbons announcing "It's a girl," not the custom ribbons they had ordered with their names on. Every box must be opened, a count done, ribbons or any print material read for accuracy, spelling, and quality. When your out-of-town guests are arriving and you are in the midst of final fittings and finishing touches, your time is going to disappear and it is essential that you have your backup and advance wedding team in place as well as your point person. Your backup wedding team is responsible for areas up to and including your wedding rehearsal. Your assigned wedding advance team and point person would oversee your wedding day requirements.

For example, on your wedding day, your point person, who will be acting on your behalf—a close friend, family member, or a hired professional—is prepared to slip away from the wedding ceremony after your vows to arrive at the reception site well in advance of your guests. There may be others helping and you need to work out the timing and logistics. One person may be required to advance the reception, another is needed to make sure all is in place for the wedding photo shoot, and both need to be taking place close to the same time. Someone else may be required to stay behind at the wedding ceremony site and collect any personal décor items if there is no supplier responsible for making sure that they are returned to you. The groom may have driven his car to the wedding ceremony site but will be transferring to the wedding photo shoot in the bride's waiting transportation and someone will need to drive his car to the reception location so it will be there for their departure.

The time to decide what they will be doing and when is now—not when you are down to the final minutes. You need them fully prepared for what exactly will be taking place, what you would like them to do, when, and in what manner. Your Wedding Flow sheets will enable you to do so easily and effortlessly.

Preparing your Wedding Flow sheets will allow you to step back and hand over responsibility with confidence so that you can relax and go into your wedding calmly, totally composed, and confident that your wedding vision is firmly in place. There may be last-minute changes that occur from areas that are beyond your control, such as heavy rains delaying a tent setup, but they will be easy to handle because everything else has been reviewed and is ready to go.

You have worked out Plan A—you have acknowledged all of your venues' and suppliers' requirements and everyone has signed off on and is working from your Wedding Flow sheets. All of your suppliers are operating from the same page—yours—and they are all informed as to what is expected. Plan B—your backup strategy in case anything unforeseen happens—is ready to go if the need arises and will not throw you into confusion and crisis mode if something unexpected hits.

Once again, you already have everything you need on hand to compile your Wedding Flow sheets. You will be referencing:

- Your Wedding Day Flow Sheets
- Your Wedding Day Blueprint
- Venue and Supplier Contracts
- Venue and Supplier Quotes

Wedding Day Contact Information

WEDDING FLOW SHEETS need to be laid out in date and time sequence. Doing this will enable you to do a cross-check to make sure that there will be no areas of overlap, all costs are captured and confirmed, and there is no outstanding information you still require.

The starting point for your Wedding Flow sheets is your venue and supplier contact information. It is essential that you have a hard copy of all the relevant names and telephone numbers. They need to be readily accessible, kept in the front of your binder, are not subject to power outages or battery failure when minutes matter most (which is why hard copy is essential), and listed in alphabetical order by category, not company name. Make extra copies available so they can be handed off to someone else easily in an emergency situation.

Start with your wedding team, follow with your venues, and lead into your wedding suppliers. While you will be familiar with who is doing what, the person you will be handing the sheets over to, who will be your venue and suppliers' main contact on your wedding day, will not. When your flowers have not arrived, they need to know exactly who to contact and how to find them quickly without alarming you by asking for the company name or information.

Wedding Party

Include each person's responsibilities (e.g., matron of honor, best man, etc.), as your point person may not personally know them. If the point person needs to find someone quickly, both the name and the role he or she is playing in your wedding party will be helpful.

Best Man

Name: _____

Address: _____

Telephone (home): _____

Telephone (cell): _____

Telephone (business): _____

Other: _____

Maid/Matron of Honor

Name: _____

Address: _____

Telephone (home): _____

Telephone (cell): _____

Telephone (business): _____

Other: _____

Ushers/Groomsmen

Name: _____

Address: _____

Telephone (home): _____

Telephone (cell): _____

Telephone (business): _____

Other: _____

Name: _____

Address: _____

Telephone (home): _____

Telephone (cell): _____

Telephone (business): _____

Other: _____

Name: _____

Address: _____

Telephone (home): _____

Telephone (cell): _____

Telephone (business): _____

Other: _____

Name: _____

Address: _____

Telephone (home): _____

Telephone (cell): _____

Telephone (business): _____

Other: _____

Name: _____

Address: _____

Telephone (home): _____

Telephone (cell): _____

Telephone (business): _____

Other: _____

Name: _____

Address: _____

Telephone (home): _____

Telephone (cell): _____

Telephone (business): _____

Other: _____

Bridesmaids

Name: _____

Address: _____

Telephone (home): _____

Telephone (cell): _____

Telephone (business): _____

Other: _____

Name: _____

Address: _____

Telephone (home): _____

Telephone (cell): _____

Telephone (business): _____

Other: _____

Name: _____

Address: _____

Telephone (home): _____

Telephone (cell): _____

Telephone (business): _____

Other: _____

Name: _____

Address: _____

Telephone (home): _____

Telephone (cell): _____

Telephone (business): _____

Other: _____

Name: _____

Address: _____

Telephone (home): _____

Telephone (cell): _____

Telephone (business): _____

Other: _____

Name: _____

Address: _____

Telephone (home): _____

Telephone (cell): _____

Telephone (business): _____

Other: _____

Bride's Parents

Name: _____

Address: _____

Telephone (home): _____

Telephone (cell): _____

Telephone (business): _____

Other: _____

Name: _____

Address: _____

Telephone (home): _____

Telephone (cell): _____

Telephone (business): _____

Other: _____

Groom's Parents

Name: _____

Address: _____

Telephone (home): _____

Telephone (cell): _____

Telephone (business): _____

Other: _____

Name: _____

Address: _____

Telephone (home): _____

Telephone (cell): _____

Telephone (business): _____

Other: _____

Officiant

Name: _____

Address: _____

Telephone (home): _____

Telephone (cell): _____

Telephone (business): _____

Other: _____

Wedding Team

List everyone who will be helping out with setup, move-in, rehearsal, wedding day, teardown and move-out.

Name: _____

Address: _____

Telephone (home): _____

Telephone (cell): _____

Telephone (business): _____

Other: _____

Name: _____

Address: _____

Telephone (home): _____

Telephone (cell): _____

Telephone (business): _____

Other: _____

Name: _____

Address: _____

Telephone (home): _____

Telephone (cell): _____

Telephone (business): _____

Other: _____

Name: _____

Address: _____

Telephone (home): _____

Telephone (cell): _____

Telephone (business): _____

Other: _____

Wedding Venues

The contact information you will require will be the same for each of these categories.

Wedding Rehearsal Dinner

List all key contacts in the order you are to deal with them. (For example, all requests may need to go through your main contact, but you need to know who the other key players are who will be in charge and on-site for your move-in, setup, rehearsal, wedding day, teardown, and move-out dates.)

Name of venue: _____

Full street address: _____

Main crossroads: _____

Main contact: _____

Title: _____

Telephone: _____

Cell phone: _____

Home telephone number in case of emergency: _____

Fax: _____

Email: _____

Other (text messaging, pager, fax, etc.): _____

Wedding Ceremony Site

List all key contacts in the order you are to deal with them. (For example, all requests may need to go through your main contact, but you need to know who the other key players are who will be in charge and on-site for your move-in, setup, rehearsal, wedding day, teardown, and move-out dates.)

Name of venue: _____

Full street address: _____

Main crossroads: _____

Main contact: _____

Title: _____

Telephone: _____

Cell phone: _____

Home telephone number in case of emergency: _____

Fax: _____

Email: _____

Other (text messaging, pager, fax, etc.): _____

Wedding Photograph Shoot Site

List all key contacts in the order you are to deal with them. (For example, all requests may need to go through your main contact, but you need to know who the other key players are who will be in charge and on-site for your move-in, setup, rehearsal, wedding day, teardown, and move-out dates.)

Name of venue: _____

Full street address: _____

Main crossroads: _____

Main contact: _____

Title: _____

Telephone: _____

Cell phone: _____

Home telephone number in case of emergency: _____

Fax: _____

Email: _____

Other (text messaging, pager, fax, etc.): _____

Name of venue: _____

Full street address: _____

Main crossroads: _____

Main contact: _____

Title: _____

Telephone: _____

Cell phone: _____

Home telephone number in case of emergency: _____

Fax: _____

Email: _____

Other (text messaging, pager, fax, etc.): _____

Wedding Reception and/or Brunch, Lunch, Afternoon Tea, or Dinner Site

List all key contacts in the order you are to deal with them. (For example, all requests may need to go through your main contact, but you need to know who the other key players are who will be in charge and on-site for your move-in, setup, rehearsal, wedding day, teardown, and move-out dates.)

Name of venue: _____

Full street address: _____

Main crossroads: _____

Main contact: _____

Title: _____

Telephone: _____

Cell phone: _____

Home telephone number in case of emergency: _____

Fax: _____

Email: _____

Other (text messaging, pager, fax, etc.): _____

Name of venue: _____

Full street address: _____

Main crossroads: _____

Main contact: _____

Title: _____

Telephone: _____

Cell phone: _____

Home telephone number in case of emergency: _____

Fax: _____

Email: _____

Other (text messaging, pager, fax, etc.): _____

Suppliers

The same contact information would be required for suppliers as venues.

Possible Supplier Categories:

- Audiovisual
- Bridal Shop
- Caterer
- Dry Cleaners
- Décor—wedding ceremony
- Décor—wedding reception
- Entertainment—wedding ceremony
- Entertainment—wedding reception
- Hairstylist
- Fire Marshal
- Florist—wedding ceremony
- Florist—wedding party
- Florist—wedding reception
- Hotel—wedding night
- Insurance
- Jeweler
- Lighting—ceremony
- Lighting—reception
- Licenses—marriage
- Makeup Artist
- Media
- Permits—fire marshal
- Permits—liquor
- Permits—road closure
- Permits—street parking
- Photographer—bride's home
- Photographer—groom's home
- Photographer—wedding ceremony

- Photographer—wedding photo shoot
- Photographer—wedding reception
- Police—escort
- Police—orange cones to block parking site with permit approval
- Police—traffic direction
- Printers—invitations, RSVP cards, thank-you cards
- Printers—place cards, printed menus, other
- Rentals
- Ropes and Stanchions
- Seamstress
- Skytrackers
- Speech Writers
- Special Effects
- Staffing
- Tent Rental
- Transportation—bride
- Transportation—groom
- Transportation—wedding party
- Travel Agency
- Tuxedo Rental
- Walkie Talkies
- Wedding Cake
- Wedding Official
- All other applicable suppliers

Wedding Schedule of Events

WHAT WILL FOLLOW next is your wedding schedule of events. Whereas your Critical Path dealt with payment schedules, contract clauses, deadlines, and overall commitments, your wedding schedule of events sheets are now moving into date and time order and will give you an overview of what everyone will be doing, when, and where—including yourself. You need to know how your wedding is laid out and where, again, you need to schedule in time buffers, even for personal errands. It is not enough for you to list a bridal fitting at 3:00 PM. You also need to factor in drive time, time to find a parking spot, walking from your car to the bridal salon, time for chit chat, last bridal fitting and gown pick up, walk to car, drive back home, estimate time for rush hour traffic, etc. You may find that when all this is taken into account, you may need to build in a time buffer of one to two hours or more. Look at moving your appointment to a time when you will not get caught up in rush hour traffic.

As carefully as you have managed your budget, you now need to manage your time so that when you arrive at the week before your wedding, you will not be overextended and continually running late. You will be on top of where you need to be and can easily amend your timing if needed. What you are doing now is giving yourself an extremely effective time and wedding management tool that will steer you away from chaos and confusion when the wedding day countdown is on. Done in a period of relative calm, you have time to plan, prepare, and plot your timelines to work to your advantage.

Your schedule of events timelines should include:

- Wedding Two Weeks Prior Schedule of Events—Overview
- Wedding Week Schedule of Events—Overview
- Wedding Rehearsal Schedule of Events—Overview
- Wedding Day Schedule of Events—Overview

Wedding Flow Sheets

YOUR WEDDING FLOW sheets are function sheets for your venues and your suppliers. Each venue and supplier and each event element under their individual responsibility is to be detailed in the time order they will take place. Each Wedding Flow page will include:

- Date
- Time
- Location
- Requirements
- Inclusions
- Special Notes/Contacts
- Costs

You can begin by setting up the framework of your Wedding Flow sheets and as details begin to unfold and information comes in, you can update them and detail your instructions.

Once you have received all information from your suppliers with regard to timing, logistics, costs, and their requirements, and transferred all information to your Wedding Flow sheets, you will have produced a script from which all your suppliers and venues can work.

Just like a stage production, once your Wedding Flow sheets or script is finished, you need to place it back in the hands of your suppliers so that they are fully apprised of what else will be taking place, what your expectations are, the delivery you require, when to enter and exit, and the part that they—and everyone involved—will be playing to produce an outstanding wedding day. Your Wedding Flow sheets can be done and distributed months ahead of your wedding date, which will leave you in a strong wedding planning position.

Once your major suppliers have received a full set of Wedding Flow sheets, they will need time to review them, advise you of any areas of concern, reconfirm the inclusions and costs you have listed, and give you written confirmation that all is in order in the outline you have delivered. Once you have received the sign of approval from your venues and suppliers and made any necessary changes to your Wedding Flow sheets, a revised copy will need to be sent to all involved. Make sure that you date your revision so that everyone knows which script they are to follow.

Minor suppliers that will not be interacting with your venue and your other suppliers, such as wedding favors that perhaps you will be having delivered to your home to be dispersed, would only require the Wedding Flow sheets that pertain to them. Suppliers that are only handling your wedding ceremony but are not involved with your wedding reception in another location only need Wedding Flow sheets that pertain to that specific part (e.g., wedding ceremony, wedding photo shoot, or wedding reception). What is important is that you keep to having everything laid out in timelines. If your wedding ceremony and wedding reception are taking place in two different locations, you may have things going on at the exact same time in two different places during move in and setup. If you need to have someone from your wedding team to oversee them, they need to know exactly what will be taking place, when, and where.

Stress Free All the Way to the Big Moment

Wedding Supplier Previews and Wedding Day Rehearsal

BETWEEN THE DATE you sent the finalized Wedding Flow sheets to your venues and suppliers and your upcoming wedding, many things will have transpired, as these two items can be months apart. In order to make sure that everything you have requested is contracted, reserved, and blocked for you; that the best possible staff are assigned to you on your wedding day; and that suppliers have had time to what they need to do, you can't wait until the last moment to send your Wedding Flow sheets in. In the interim, there may be staff changes, a supplier may have changed their direction and focus, there could have been a change of hands and new ownership, and hundreds of other special events and weddings to quote on, prepare for, and produce.

As your wedding is approaching, you now want your wedding in the front of your suppliers' and venues' minds. The way that you accomplish this and ensure that everything you contracted and requested is still in place is by doing a wedding day pre-event meeting with your suppliers and venues. This is a step no professional special event or wedding planner would miss. It is *their* must-have and should become one of your must-haves as well. A pre-event meeting is something that venues and suppliers do every day with the professional industry as a matter of course.

Another reason the pre-event wedding review is essential is that in many cases, your actual wedding day on-site coordination will be turned over to someone who handles that aspect of the supplier's or venue's business, so once again your file will be changing hands. At your wedding pre-event or wedding day dress rehearsal meeting—with each supplier and venue—you can request that the person who will be handling or overseeing your wedding be present.

There are several ways that you can conduct your wedding day rehearsal and you will need to look at the way that best meets your needs and the needs of your suppliers. How and where you set up your meetings will depend on whether or not your wedding ceremony and reception are taking place in one location or two separate facilities and if there are two entirely different sets of suppliers—some involved in only the wedding ceremony and others handling the wedding reception, or if there is crossover and they are involved in both.

The best scenario is to hold your meeting at the wedding ceremony or wedding reception site. You can have a private meeting with your venue and then either have all your suppliers join the meeting or schedule them one after the other. Some may only need to sit in for a short while (e.g., if they are only handling centerpieces), while others whose areas of responsibility are interconnected may find it advisable to be there for the entire time. You will need to be respectful of their time constraints. Your venue may have a room that you can use for your meeting at no charge or they may levy a charge for room rental and any refreshments that are served.

Holding your wedding day rehearsal meeting at the venue allows you to be in one location, not all over town meeting with suppliers individually. If anyone needs a walk-through of the loading dock to see if there have been any changes since their initial site inspection or to refresh their memory, you are already there. They have the people in the room from the venue who can answer any questions that may arise immediately.

If your suppliers cannot meet at your venues (e.g., because of travel time or other concerns), another consideration is to have the meeting at a location convenient to all of you. However, make the location as convenient for you as possible so you are not spending hours in traffic and so you have easy access to wedding planning material that you may require (e.g., past correspondence). For your venues, it is important that you make the time to meet with them and walk the property to make sure that you don't encounter any surprises. If at all possible, your caterer; décor company; and audiovisual, staging, and lighting companies should meet at the site as well. You are not likely to get your musicians to attend, but if you have contracted their services through an entertainment management company, they will most often send a representative and/or one of the technical crew.

It is recommended to hold your wedding day rehearsal meeting two to four weeks before your wedding. To prepare for your meeting you will need to make sure that all the people attending have all received and reviewed your wedding flow sheets. You will also want to have your point person with you at the meeting so that they and your suppliers can put names to faces and know who to go to immediately should they require assistance. Your suppliers also need to know that this person will be acting in your stead on your wedding day. If suppliers require any additional information after this meeting from you or on your wedding day, they are to contact or go through your point person as they are be handling all on-site orchestration for you. Your suppliers need to know that this person has your permission to make any necessary changes that may be required. If any of these changes are going to involve additional dollars being spent, you need to address this with your suppliers up front as to how you want this handled (e.g., they discuss it with your point person and they in turn present it to you, etc.).

This is not the time to bring your wedding team in. That will be done at the next step. To bring them in now would only serve to confuse them; they only need to focus on their final directives after your meeting with your suppliers. Their help at this time may be better spent on working on your seating chart, cross-checking names on place cards with seating assignments, putting them in alphabetical order so that they can be quickly set out at the reception, etc., and all the other finishing touches that are also essential to pull off a polished wedding day production.

It is important that you lead the meeting and that you make sure all the areas that you deem important are covered. Work your way through the Wedding Flow sheets with your suppliers in date and time sequence. It is important that you don't get pulled off topic. Jot down anything that comes up in the meeting that needs to be addressed and get back to it once you have finished your review. Have your point person take notes on any changes. When you are busy answering and asking questions, it is easy to miss an important point. Ask suppliers to bring any prepared internal function sheets they may have ready for your review. You will also need them to bring copies of any outstanding permits and insurance documents that may be needed. It is important to have a copy of them in your wedding planner in case they have to be produced immediately on your wedding day. While the suppliers should have a copy of them as well, having backup is always advisable. Police and fire marshals can and have closed down special events—including weddings—when the proper paperwork was not available.

The purpose of your wedding day rehearsal is to serve as a cross-check that everything has been done, nothing has been overlooked, and there is nothing you need to be advised of that you don't already know (e.g., renovations are now taking place or there are talks of a strike). It is a meeting where planning and preparation come together with wedding day presentation. How your wedding is delivered is as important as the elements that come together to create your wedding vision and a final walk-through and review should never be optional.

Your wedding day rehearsal is a key finishing touch to your wedding day. It is *your* wedding day and *you* are the client. Leave no question unasked. Remember to be focused on delivery, presentation, and your wedding day vision.

Like Clockwork

On-Site Wedding Day Orchestration

ON YOUR WEDDING day, you will not be in a position to orchestrate your wedding. You will be stepping into the starring role and it is important to hand off responsibility so that you can enjoy your wedding day.

In the months before your wedding, you will have brought your point person into your plans. She (or he) has sat in on your wedding day rehearsal meetings and is now up to speed on how and when things should process. She will be the one leading your wedding team, signing off items (such as your bar bill) after comparing costs to your Wedding Flow sheets, and physically seeing what you are being charged for (e.g., opened bottles and advising staff when to slow down or close off bar service based on your instructions). She has a huge role to play on your wedding day—that role is no longer yours. You can't be standing at the altar fretting about whether or not the caterer has arrived on time at your wedding reception. You will spoil your wedding day if you do. You have given your best to the planning, preparation, and expected presentation, but now as your wedding rapidly approaches, it is time to let go and place your wedding dreams into trusted hands.

What you will want to do now is invite your wedding team to a meeting where you will be officially handing your responsibility to the person who will be handling on-site orchestration and who will relay your wedding team's timing and responsibilities. Any questions the wedding team may have in the upcoming days need to go directly to him or her. If you step back into the role of wedding planner, you may unintention-ally leave your key person out of the loop. Questions need to go through your point person—and if you receive any request directly, you must steer that person back to asking your point person. You may need to reinforce this and not be drawn in. You need to deal only with or through your point person at this stage.

When you schedule a meeting with your wedding team, allow sufficient time to answer their initial flurry of questions. The more your wedding team knows about your wedding day and how it is to unfold, the better they can step in to help in other areas if needed.

You will need to prepare for letting go by scheduling in the personal activities that now require your attention. These can be pampering (such as a manicure or pedicure for the bride and groom), sightseeing with your out-of-town guests, packing for your honey-moon, other special last-minute details, or even time to enjoy a favorite pursuit. That way when you hand off your responsibility, you have a host of other things to look forward to that are all part of your wedding experience.

Letting Go—Handing Off Responsibility

- Schedule personal activities to take place immediately after you have handed off your wedding planning duties and make sure to include ones that will be relaxing.
- Plan a wedding team meeting and officially hand off responsibility.
- Distribute Wedding Flow sheets and relevant information to your team.
- Direct everyone to go to your point person if they have any questions.
- Take time to enjoy the remaining time as an engaged couple.
- Schedule an activity—full of love and laughter—for when you return for those closest to you so you can take in their wedding day memories and share yours with them.

After the Wedding

ONE AREA COUPLES often overlook is planning for *after* the honeymoon. For months you have been planning and looking forward to your wedding day and honeymoon, and when those days have come and gone, there is often post-wedding letdown. It's not letdown in your wedding, but everything has come to an end, all the planning and preparation, anticipation, and experiencing have come and gone. For so long it has been a part of your life and while you are moving forward to a new chapter in your life, the initial few days after you return from your wedding or honeymoon can feel restless until you settle into your new life together.

It can feel is as though you have been climbing a mountain of energy and excitement with your wedding and honeymoon being the pinnacle and all of a sudden it stops with a grand finale. Professional special event and wedding planners experience this regularly, and it is not even their wedding! Some make it a rule to do nothing the day after an event but savor the feelings and recapture the memories they helped to create. As the bride, your feelings are so intense during the final weeks as your wedding counts down, when you are focused on making everything as memorable, meaningful, and magical as possible, and then it is over. There are still bills to be paid, thank-you notes to be written, wedding photographs to savor, and new exciting moments to come. If you put something in place for when you return, you keep the momentum going. You want to return rested and recharged and have something already in place to look forward to. When you return, your families and friends are going to be anxious to hear about your honeymoon and to see your wedding photos. Making plans for some casual upcoming events will give you something else to look forward to. Your guests are going to want to share their experiences of your wedding day with you as well. Share stories and anecdotes and, if you can, bring them all together again in a lighthearted way soon after your return—you will get to enjoy it while the moment is fresh in everyone's memory.

Conclusion

YOU HAVE NOW created a dream wedding that defines you as a couple. You have stayed focused on your wedding vision and your must-haves, and been financially responsible to yourself and to others.

Wrapping your wedding in layers of what held special meaning to you is what, when you look back, will be what was most memorable and magical about your special day. If anything did happen that you could not have prevented, it will not linger on in your memories or in the minds of your wedding guests. It will simply be a part of the whole wedding experience. At that point, you just go forward. No one notices because they are focused on the big picture—the love shining between the couple.

When you plan your wedding, it is important to pay attention to detail and focus on each element. But on your wedding day, you need to let go. You have poured your heart and soul into creating your dream wedding. You can now relax. You have done all that you possibly can and now it is time to enjoy the big picture and capture the essence of what this day is truly about—a celebration with close family and friends of your love and your commitment to one another.

Wedding Planning Forms and Checklists

Wedding Flow Sheet 176
Vendor Comparison Chart 178

Use this chart for each type of vendor you are hiring for your wedding. Make a separate copy to compare wedding consultants, print material suppliers, ceremony sites, florists, photographers, videographers, reception sites, caterers, bakeries, entertainment or music companies, transportation companies, and wedding dress and tuxedo choices.

Your Wedding Dress 179
Payment and Deposit Tracker. 180
License and Legalities 184
Printed Material Checklist 185
Wedding Party & Family Attire Checklist (Female) 186
Wedding Party & Family Attire Checklist (Male) 187
Wedding Party & Family Floral Requirements 188
Menu Worksheet 189
Wedding Song List Worksheet 190
Shower Worksheet and Checklist. 192
Accommodations 194
Transportation 195
Photography and Videography Checklist 196
Final Guest Seating Chart 198
Wedding Day Checklist 200
Calendar 201

❧ Wedding Flow Overview Worksheet

Date: _____   Date: _____   Date: _____

Day: _____   Day: _____   Day: _____

Early AM

5:00 AM   _____   _____   _____

6:00 AM   _____   _____   _____

Morning

7:00 AM   _____   _____   _____

8:00 AM   _____   _____   _____

9:00 AM   _____   _____   _____

10:00 AM   _____   _____   _____

11:00 AM   _____   _____   _____

Midday

12:00 PM   _____   _____   _____

Afternoon

1:00 PM   _____   _____   _____

2:00 PM   _____   _____   _____

3:00 PM   _____   _____   _____

4:00 PM   _____   _____   _____

5:00 PM   _____   _____   _____

Early PM

6:00 PM   _____   _____   _____

7:00 PM   _____   _____   _____

Evening

8:00 PM   _____   _____   _____

9:00 PM   _____   _____   _____

10:00 PM   _____   _____   _____

11:00 PM   _____   _____   _____

12:00 AM   _____   _____   _____

Date: _____   Date: _____   Date: _____

Day: _____   Day: _____   Day: _____

Early AM

5:00 AM   _____   _____   _____

6:00 AM   _____   _____   _____

Morning

7:00 AM   _____   _____   _____

8:00 AM   _____   _____   _____

9:00 AM   _____   _____   _____

10:00 AM   _____   _____   _____

11:00 AM   _____   _____   _____

Midday

12:00 PM   _____   _____   _____

Afternoon

1:00 PM   _____   _____   _____

2:00 PM   _____   _____   _____

3:00 PM   _____   _____   _____

4:00 PM   _____   _____   _____

5:00 PM   _____   _____   _____

Early PM

6:00 PM   _____   _____   _____

7:00 PM   _____   _____   _____

Evening

8:00 PM   _____   _____   _____

9:00 PM   _____   _____   _____

10:00 PM   _____   _____   _____

11:00 PM   _____   _____   _____

12:00 AM   _____   _____   _____

❧ Vendor Comparison Chart

	Possibility One	Possibility Two	Possibility Three
Company Name:			
Contact Information: (contact name, address, phone, etc.)			
General Description of Style and Services:			
Positive Attributes:			
Negative Attributes:			
Estimated Total Cost:			

❧ Your Wedding Dress

Retailer: _____

Contact: _____

Contact Info (address, phone number, etc.):

_____

_____

_____

Designer: _____

Dress Description (sleeveless, empire waist, etc.):

_____

_____

Size: _____

Cost: _____

	First Fitting	Second Fitting	Final Fitting
Date:			
Time:			
Alteration Description:			
Alteration Cost:			

Final Pickup Date: _____

Accessories
- ☐ Shoes
- ☐ Stockings
- ☐ Headpiece/Veil
- ☐ Purse
- ☐ Jewelry

✿ Payment and Deposit Tracker

	Total Cost	Deposit Amount and Date	Second Payment Due	Third Payment Due	Final Payment Due

Wedding Consultant

Consultant Name and Phone: _____ Contract Date: _____					

Stationer

Business Name and Phone: _____ Contract Date: _____					

Calligrapher

Business Name and Phone: _____ Contract Date: _____					

Ceremony Site

Site Name and Phone: _____ Contract Date: _____					

Wedding Gown

Store Name and Phone: _____ Contract Date: _____					

Tuxedo Rental

Store Name and Phone: _____ Contract Date: _____					

	Total Cost	Deposit Amount and Date	Second Payment Due	Third Payment Due	Final Payment Due

Florist

Business Name and Phone: _____

Contract Date: _____

Photographer

Business Name and Phone: _____

Contract Date: _____

Videographer

Business Name and Phone: _____

Contract Date: _____

Decorations

Business Name and Phone: _____

Contract Date: _____

Rehearsal Dinner

Site Name and Phone: _____

Contract Date: _____

Reception Site

Site Name and Phone: _____

Contract Date: _____

	Total Cost	Deposit Amount and Date	Second Payment Due	Third Payment Due	Final Payment Due
Caterer					
Business Name and Phone: _____ Contract Date: _____					
Liquor Services					
Business Name and Phone: _____ Contract Date: _____					
Bakery					
Business Name and Phone: _____ Contract Date: _____					
Music—Ceremony					
Business Name and Phone: _____ Contract Date: _____					
Music—Reception					
Business Name and Phone: _____ Contract Date: _____					
Party Favors					
Business Name and Phone: _____ Contract Date: _____					

	Total Cost	Deposit Amount and Date	Second Payment Due	Third Payment Due	Final Payment Due

Gift Suppliers

Business Name and Phone: _____ Contract Date: _____					

Valet Services

Business Name and Phone: _____ Contract Date: _____					

Transportation

Business Name and Phone: _____ Contract Date: _____					

Rentals and Supplies

Business Name and Phone: _____ Contract Date: _____					

Marriage License

Office Address: _____

Contact Name(s): _____

Contact Number(s): _____

Appointment Date & Time: _____

Cost: _____

Additional Copies: _____

Waiting Period: _____

Requirements

Requirements vary from state to state. For more complete information, visit your county clerk's office.

- Age
- Proof of residency
- Blood tests
- Witnesses for signing application (Maid of Honor and Best Man)
- Proof of citizenship (U.S. or foreign)
- Proof of previous marriage (if applicable)
- Letters of parental consent (minors only, age varies by state)
- Tax information

Notify of Change of Address and/or Name Change

☐ Post Office
☐ Insurance Policies
☐ Driver's License
☐ Passport
☐ Social Security Card
☐ Medical Records
☐ Tax Forms
☐ Phone Company and Other Utilities
☐ Employee Records
☐ Deeds, Mortgages, and Leases
☐ Banks and Other Financial Institutions
☐ Voter Registration
☐ Wills
☐ Credit Card Companies
☐ Stocks and Investment Funds

☐ Schools and Alumni Associations
☐ Magazine Subscriptions
☐ Mailing Lists
☐ Music/Movie Club Memberships
☐ Club Memberships (gyms, etc.)
☐ Store Memberships (warehouse clubs, etc.)
☐ Update Email Address
☐ Update Email Contacts
☐ Website List Serves

Invitations

	Item Required	Quantity Required	Ordered	Received
Save the Date Cards				
Save the Date Envelopes				
Wedding Invitations				
Wedding Invitation Envelopes				
RSVP Cards				
RSVP Envelopes				
Out-of-town Guest Information Cards				
Wedding Itinerary Inserts				
Wedding & Reception Map Insert				
Parking Validation or Instruction Insert				
Other:				

Wedding Ceremony

Reserved Parking Cards				
Pew Cards				
Wedding Ceremony Programs				
Other:				

Wedding Reception & Dinner

Table Seating Place Cards				
Table Identification Cards (e.g., Table # or Name)				
Name Cards at Table				
Printed Menus				
Other (Printed napkins, cake boxes, favor tags):				
Thank-You Cards				

❧ Wedding Party & Family Attire Checklist (Female)

Each female member of the wedding party and/or family requires a separate page.

Name: _____

Role: _____

Address for Pick Up on Wedding Day:

_____

Contact Number(s):

_____

_____

Personal Info

Dress Size: _____

Bust: _____

Waist: _____

Hips: _____

Shoe Size: _____

Hat Size: _____

Glove Size: _____

Shoe Size: _____

Color Scheme: _____

Wedding Attire

Store/Rental: _____

Sales Contact: _____

Contact Numbers: _____

Description of Attire: _____

Store: _____

Sales Contact: _____

Contact Numbers: _____

Description of Attire: _____

Date Ordered: _____

Deposit Paid: _____

Balance To Be Paid: _____

First Fitting Date: _____

Second Fitting Date: _____

Pick Up Date: _____

Return Date: _____

Final Attire Checklist

☐ Dress Picked Up

☐ Shoes Picked Up

☐ Hat or Headpiece Picked Up

☐ Gloves Picked Up

☐ Flowers Ordered

☐ Transportation Arranged to Ceremony, Wedding Photos, Reception, and Home

☐ Scheduled Makeup and Hair Appointment

Each male member of the wedding party and/or family requires a separate page.

Name: _____

Role: _____

Address for Pick Up on Wedding Day:

_____

Contact Number(s):

_____

_____

Personal Info

Jacket Size: _____

Shirt Size: _____

Neck: _____

Sleeve: _____

Pant Size: _____

Waist: _____

Inseam: _____

Out Seam: _____

Shoe Size: _____

Color Scheme: _____

Wedding Attire

Store/Rental: _____

Sales Contact: _____

Contact Numbers: _____

Description of Attire: _____

Store: _____

Sales Contact: _____

Contact Numbers: _____

Description of Attire: _____

Date Ordered: _____

Deposit Paid: _____

Balance To Be Paid: _____

First Fitting Date: _____

Second Fitting Date: _____

Pick Up Date: _____

Return Date: _____

Final Attire Checklist

☐ Suit/Tux Picked Up

☐ Shoes Picked Up

☐ Shirt Picked Up

☐ Tie, Belt, Cuff Links, etc. Picked Up

☐ Flowers Ordered

☐ Transportation Arranged to Ceremony, Wedding, Photos, Reception, & Home

☐ Hair & Grooming Appointments Scheduled

Bride

	Item Required	Quantity Required	Ordered	Received
Bouquet				
Floral Headpiece				
Separate Bouquet for Throwing to Guests				
Going Away Corsage or Wristlet				
Honor Attendant Bouquet or Boutonniere				
Attendants' Bouquets or Boutonnieres				
Flower Girl Bouquet				

Groom

	Item Required	Quantity Required	Ordered	Received
Boutonniere				
Best Man's Boutonniere				
Groomsmen's Boutonnieres				
Ushers' Boutonnieres				
Ring Bearer Boutonniere				
Corsages (Mother of Bride/Groom, Grandmothers, etc.)				
Boutonnieres (Father of Bride/Groom, Grandfathers, etc.)				
Wedding Officiant				

	Selection One	Selection Two	Selection Three
Cocktail Party			
Hors d'oeuvres			
Description			
Cost			

Reception

Appetizer			
Salad			
Main Course			
Cost Per Person			
Dessert Options			
Description			
Cost			

Alcohol

	Wine	Champagne	Liquor
Selections			
Quantity Needed			
Hours Served			
Cost			

Total Number of Reception Guests: _____

Total Alcohol Cost: _____

Total Menu Cost: _____

❧ Wedding Song List Worksheet

	Song Title	Artist/Performed By
Ceremony		
Prelude		
Seating of Parents		
Processional		
Bride's Entrance		
Ceremony		
Solo		
Solo		
Solo		
Recessional		

Reception		
Introduction		
First Dance		
Father and Daughter Dance		
Mother and Son Dance		
Bridal Party Dance		
Other Important Songs:		

Other Songs to Play During Reception

Song Title	Artist/Performed By

Do Not Play List

Include the songs that SHOULD NOT be played at your wedding.

Song Title	Artist/Performed By

❧ Shower Worksheet and Checklist

Copy this form as many times as needed to accommodate your list of guests. Forms can be given to those hosting the party and returned to you when you're ready to send out thank-you cards.

Host

Name: _____

Address: _____

Contact Number(s): _____

Date: _____

Time: _____

Theme: _____

Guest Name(s):

_____

_____

☐ Invitation Sent

☐ RSVP Received

Address:

_____

Of Guests _____

Contact Number(s):

_____

Gift Description:

Relationship to Bride/Groom:

_____

_____

_____

Special Notes/Meals:

☐ Thank-You Card Sent

_____

Guest Name(s):

_____

_____

☐ Invitation Sent

☐ RSVP Received

Address:

_____

Of Guests _____

Contact Number(s):

_____

Gift Description:

Relationship to Bride/Groom:

_____

_____

_____

Special Notes/Meals:

☐ Thank-You Card Sent

_____

Guest Name(s):

_____

_____

Address:

_____

Contact Number(s):

_____

Relationship to Bride/Groom:

_____

Special Notes/Meals:

_____

☐ Invitation Sent
☐ RSVP Received

Of Guests _____
Gift Description:

_____

_____

☐ Thank-You Card Sent

Guest Name(s):

_____

_____

Address:

_____

Contact Number(s):

_____

Relationship to Bride/Groom:

_____

Special Notes/Meals:

_____

☐ Invitation Sent
☐ RSVP Received

Of Guests _____
Gift Description:

_____

_____

☐ Thank-You Card Sent

Guest Name(s):

_____

_____

Address:

_____

Contact Number(s):

_____

Relationship to Bride/Groom:

_____

Special Notes/Meals:

_____

☐ Invitation Sent
☐ RSVP Received

Of Guests _____
Gift Description:

_____

_____

☐ Thank-You Card Sent

Make additional copies as needed for each member of the bridal party, family, and out-of-town guests.

Hotel Information

	Option 1	Option 2	Option 3
Name			
Address			
Contact Number(s)			
Fax			
Website			
Reservation Deadline			
Confirmation Number			
Number of Rooms			
Rate			

Make additional copies as needed for each member of the bridal party, family, and out-of-town guests.

Company Information

	Option 1	Option 2	Option 3
Name			
Address			
Contact Number(s)			
Fax			
Website			
Reservation Deadline			
Confirmation Number			
Fare			

Photography and Videography Checklist

Photographer: _____

Business Name: _____

Address: _____

Contact Number(s): _____

Cost: _____

Contractual Agreements or Conditions: _____

_____

Pre-Ceremony Photographs:

☐ Bride getting dressed

☐ Attendants getting dressed

☐ Putting on garter

☐ Bride with parents

☐ Bride with maid/matron of honor

☐ Bride with bridesmaids

☐ Bride with the flower girl or ring bearer

☐ Groom dressing

☐ Groomsmen dressing

☐ Putting on boutonniere

☐ Groom with parents

☐ Groom with best man

☐ Groom with groomsmen

☐ Groom with ring bearer

☐ Bride and her father before
   the processional

☐ Groom before the processional

☐ Others: _____

☐ Others: _____

Ceremony Photographs:

☐ Guests arriving

☐ Seating of groom's parents

☐ Seating of bride's parents

☐ Groom at end of aisle

☐ Processional

☐ Giving the bride away

☐ Bride and groom saying their vows

☐ Musicians, soloists, readers

☐ Exchange of rings

☐ Kiss at the altar

☐ Recessional

☐ Others: _____

☐ Others: _____

Formal Photographs:

- ☐ Bride alone
- ☐ Bride and groom
- ☐ Bride, groom, and officiant
- ☐ Bride with her mother
- ☐ Bride with her father
- ☐ Bride with her parents
- ☐ Bride with her family
- ☐ Bride with her maid of honor
- ☐ Bride with her attendants
- ☐ Flower girls and ring bearers
- ☐ Groom alone
- ☐ Groom with his mother
- ☐ Groom with his father
- ☐ Groom with his parents
- ☐ Groom with his family
- ☐ Groom and the best man
- ☐ Groom and his attendants
- ☐ Entire wedding party
- ☐ Bride, groom, maid of honor, and best man
- ☐ Bride and groom with both sets of parents
- ☐ Bride and groom with bride's family
- ☐ Bride and groom with groom's family
- ☐ Others: _____

Reception Photographs:

- ☐ Bride and groom entering the reception
- ☐ Receiving line
- ☐ Guests
- ☐ Cake
- ☐ Tables and décor
- ☐ Favors
- ☐ Bride and groom's first dance
- ☐ Musicians
- ☐ Dancing
- ☐ Cake cutting
- ☐ Toasts
- ☐ Bouquet toss
- ☐ Garter toss
- ☐ Bride and groom leaving the reception
- ☐ Decorated Car
- ☐ Others: _____

Videographer

Name: _____

Telephone: _____

Address: _____

Email: _____

Cost: _____

Contractual Conditions and Agreements: _____

_____

R=Reception (Light Food & Beverages Pre-Meal)   M=Meal (Sit-Down Service Following Reception)

# Of Guests R	# Of Guests M	# Of Tables of 6	# Of Tables of 8	# Of Tables of 10	# At Head Table
_____	_____	_____	_____	_____	_____

Table # _____

1. _____
2. _____
3. _____
4. _____
5. _____
6. _____
7. _____
8. _____
9. _____
10. _____
Special Notes: _____

Table # _____

1. _____
2. _____
3. _____
4. _____
5. _____
6. _____
7. _____
8. _____
9. _____
10. _____
Special Notes: _____

Table # _____

1. _____
2. _____
3. _____
4. _____
5. _____
6. _____
7. _____
8. _____
9. _____
10. _____
Special Notes: _____

Table # _____

1. _____
2. _____
3. _____
4. _____
5. _____
6. _____
7. _____
8. _____
9. _____
10. _____
Special Notes: _____

Table # _____

1. _____
2. _____
3. _____
4. _____
5. _____
6. _____
7. _____
8. _____
9. _____
10. _____
Special Notes: _____

Table # _____

1. _____
2. _____
3. _____
4. _____
5. _____
6. _____
7. _____
8. _____
9. _____
10. _____
Special Notes: _____

Table # _____

1. _____
2. _____
3. _____
4. _____
5. _____
6. _____
7. _____
8. _____
9. _____
10. _____
Special Notes: _____

Table # _____

1. _____
2. _____
3. _____
4. _____
5. _____
6. _____
7. _____
8. _____
9. _____
10. _____
Special Notes: _____

Wedding Day Checklist

Wedding Ceremony

Bride   Groom

Bride	Groom	
☐	☐	Marriage License
☐	☐	Any Additional Required Documentation
☐	☐	Bride's Wedding Band
☐	☐	Groom's Wedding Band
☐	☐	Payment Envelopes/Checks
☐	☐	Other: _____

Personal Care Pouch

☐ Aspirin or other pain reliever
☐ Breath Mints
☐ First Aid
☐ Bottled Water*
☐ Clear Nail Polish (for runs, etc.)*
☐ Comb
☐ Contact Solution
☐ Contact Case
☐ Cotton Balls
☐ Deodorant*
☐ Energy Bars
☐ Extension Cord
☐ Extra Panty Hose
☐ Feminine Products
☐ Glasses
☐ Going-Away Outfit/Clothes
☐ Hair Brush
☐ Hair Pins and Hair Accessories
☐ Hairspray*
☐ Hand Mirror
☐ Handkerchief
☐ Hand Sanitizer
☐ Honeymoon Documents and Suitcases
☐ Keys
☐ Kleenex
☐ Lint Roller

☐ Lip Balm
☐ Makeup for Touchups*
☐ Makeup Removal*
☐ Markers, Highlighters, Glue Sticks*
☐ Medication (upset stomach, decongestant, etc.)*
☐ Mini Stapler, Paper Punch, Scissors
☐ Moist Towlettes
☐ Nail File
☐ Nail Polish*
☐ Nail Polish Remover*
☐ Nail Glue (in case of a broken nail)*
☐ Pencils, Pens, String, Rubber Bands, etc.
☐ Perfume/Cologne*
☐ Q-tips
☐ Safety Pins
☐ Scarf (to protect dress from makeup)
☐ Shoes (comfortable)
☐ Socks (for groomsmen)
☐ Static Cling Remover
☐ Styptic Pencil
☐ Sunscreen*
☐ Supply of quarters
☐ Tape (regular, masking, and electrical)
☐ Thumbtacks, Push Pins, String, Elastics
☐ Travel or Steam Iron
☐ Writing Pads and Post-It® Notes

*Remember to pack anything that can stain or leak in plastic bags

Month: _____   Year: _____

Monday	Tuesday	Wednesday	Thursday	Friday	Saturday	Sunday

Month: _____   Year: _____

Monday	Tuesday	Wednesday	Thursday	Friday	Saturday	Sunday

Month: _____   Year: _____

Monday	Tuesday	Wednesday	Thursday	Friday	Saturday	Sunday

Month: _____   Year: _____

Monday	Tuesday	Wednesday	Thursday	Friday	Saturday	Sunday

Month: _____ Year: _____

Monday	Tuesday	Wednesday	Thursday	Friday	Saturday	Sunday

Month: _____   Year: _____

Monday	Tuesday	Wednesday	Thursday	Friday	Saturday	Sunday

Month: _____   Year: _____

Monday	Tuesday	Wednesday	Thursday	Friday	Saturday	Sunday

Month: _____   Year: _____

Monday	Tuesday	Wednesday	Thursday	Friday	Saturday	Sunday

Month: _____   Year: _____

Monday	Tuesday	Wednesday	Thursday	Friday	Saturday	Sunday

Month: _____   Year: _____

Monday	Tuesday	Wednesday	Thursday	Friday	Saturday	Sunday

Month: _____   Year: _____

Monday	Tuesday	Wednesday	Thursday	Friday	Saturday	Sunday

Month: _____   Year: _____

Monday	Tuesday	Wednesday	Thursday	Friday	Saturday	Sunday

Index

Beverages, 101
  Beers, Guide to, 103
  Champagne, Guide to, 101
  Questions to Ask, 105
  Quick Stats and Facts, 106
  Requirements, Determining
    Your, 101
  What They Need to Know,
    103
  What to Look For, 106
  What to Watch Out For, 106
  Wines, Guide to, 102
Blueprint, Your Wedding, 39
  Creating, 39
  Wedding Flow Breakdown, 43
  What to Include, 42
Centerpieces, 91
  Requirements, Determining
    Your, 93
Contract Negotiations, 130
  Agreement of Terms, 138
  Cancellation, 131
  Coat Check Clauses, 136
  Delivery Clauses, 136
  Finalizing, 138
  Guest Guarantee, 133
  Insurance and Protection of
    Property Clauses, 137
  Payment Schedule, 132
  Preferred Caterers and
    Suppliers Clauses, 134
  Service Staff Clauses, 135
Critical Path, 141, 142, 151
Decision Making, 19
  What Matters Most, 20
    Guest List, 20
    Wedding Reception
      Inclusions, 26
      Audio, 28
      Décor, 27
      Entertainment, 28
      Food & Beverage, 26

Lighting, 28
Location, 26
Management Fees, 29
Negotiation, 29
Staging, 28
Visual, 28
Wedding Suppliers, 29
Wedding Reception Styles,
  25
Wedding Venue, 24
Décor Company, 85
  Questions to Ask, 87
  Requirements, Determining
    Your, 86
  Special Considerations, 89
  What They Need to Know, 87
  What to Look For, 88
  What to Watch Out For, 88
Delegating, 172
Elements of Wedding, The, 2
Emotion of Wedding, The, 8
Energy of Wedding, The, 8
Environment of Wedding, The, 5
  Wedding Day Style, 7
  Wedding Day Venue, 5
    Budget Considerations, 7
    Date, 5
    Indoor or Outdoor Affair,
      6
    Location, 5
    Season, 6
    Separate Facilities, 7
    Time of Day, 6
Essentials of Wedding, The, 4
Finishing Touches, 115
  Bridal Attire, 117
  First Night Accommodation,
    118
  Groom's Attire, 117
  Hairstylist, 117
  Honeymoon, 119
  Makeup, 118

Personal Items, 118
Wedding Cake, 116
  Cost Considerations, 116
  Critical Advance
    Information, 116
  Special Considerations,
    116
Wedding Favors, 117
Wedding Party Attire, 117
Wedding Party Gifts, 118
Wedding Rings, 118
Floral Arrangements, 89
  Information, 91
  Questions to Ask, 90
  Requirements, Determining
    Yours, 89
  What They Need to Know, 90
  What to Look For, 91
  What to Watch Out For, 91
Food, 95
  Buffet, 96
    Sit-Down Buffet, 97
    Stand-Up Buffet, 97
  Considerations, 96
  Considerations for Children,
    98
  Questions to Ask, 99
  Requirements, Determining
    Your, 95
  Sit-Down Dinner, 98
  What They Need to Know, 98
  What to Look For, 99
  What to Watch Out For, 100
Honeymoon, After the, 172
Invitations, 78
  Mailing Considerations, 80
  Requirements, How to
    Determine, 78
  Special Considerations, 82
  Timeline Considerations, 80
  What to Look For, 81
  What to Watch Out For, 81

Music and Entertainment, 108
    Information, 110
    Questions to Ask, 109
    Quick Stats and Facts, 112
    Special Considerations, 111
    What They Need to Know,
        109
    What to Look For, 111
    What to Watch Out For, 111
Photography, 113
    Questions to Ask, 114
    Special Considerations, 115
    What They Need to Know, 114
    What to Look For, 115
    What to Watch Out For, 115
Proposal, Written, 119
    Request for Proposal
        Directions, 120
Rental Company, 93
    Questions to Ask, 94
    Site Inspection, 95
    What They Need to Know,
        93
    What to Look For, 94
    What to Watch Out For, 95
Rentals, 107
    Information, 108
    Questions to Ask, 107
    Requirements, Determining
        Your, 107
    Special Considerations, 108
    What They Need to Know,
        107
    What to Look For, 108
    What to Watch Out For, 108
Schedule of Events, 164
Site, Finding the Perfect, 49
    Contract, Finalizing the, 69
    Cost Comparison, 68
    Information Necessary, 65
    Inspection, 68
    Research Tips, 64, 69
    Second Option, 50
    Tentative Hold, 50
    Venue Requirements, 50
Staging Needs, 112
    Lighting, 112

Questions to Ask, 113
    What They Need to Know,
        112
Step 1: Visualize Your Wedding
    Day Dreams, 1–18
Step 2: Focusing on What Matters
    Most, 19–38
Step 3: Designing Your Realistic
    Blueprint, 39–48
Step 4: Choosing the Perfect
    Wedding and Reception Site,
    49–72
Step 5: Selecting the Right
    Wedding Vendors, 73–126
Step 6: Staying Centered About
    Finances, 127–140
Step 7: Creating Your Critical
    Path, 141–152
Step 8: Wedding Flow Sheets,
    153–166
Step 9: Wedding Supplier
    Previews & Wedding Day
    Rehearsal, 167–170
Step 10: On-Site Wedding Day
    Orchestration, 171–174
Transportation, 82
    Information, 84
    Questions to Ask, 84
    Requirements, Determining
        Your, 83
    Special Considerations, 85
    What They Need to Know, 84
    What to Look For, 85
    What to Watch Out For, 85
Wedding Flow Sheets, 164
Worksheets
    Accommodations, 194
    Final Guest Seating Chart,
        198–199
    Guest List, 22–23
    Wedding Flow Overview
        Worksheet, 176–177
    License and Legalities, 184
    Menu Worksheet, 189
    Our Shared Wedding Vision,
        30–37

Payment and Deposit Tracker,
    180–183
Photography and Videography
    Checklist, 196–197
Printed Material Checklist,
    185
Questionnaire for Each
    Venue, 66–67
Questions to Ask Prospective
    Suppliers, 76–77
Quick Overview of Possible
    Wedding Event Elements
    and Price Considerations,
    123–124
Shower Worksheet and
    Checklist, 192–193
Supplier's Information
    Worksheet, 75
Transportation, 195
Vendor Comparison Chart,
    178
Wedding Ceremony and
    Reception Requirements
    Questionnaire, 51–63
Wedding Critical Path
    Worksheet, 144–148
Wedding Day Blueprint,
    46–48
Wedding Day Checklist, 200
Wedding Party & Family Attire
    Checklist (Female), 186
Wedding Party & Family Attire
    Checklist (Male), 187
Wedding Party & Family Floral
    Requirements, 188
Wedding Song List Worksheet,
    190–191
Wedding Venue and Supplier
    Contact Sheet, 157–163
Wedding Vision
    Questionnaire, 10–18
Your Wedding Dress, 179

This book is dedicated with much love to my Mom and Dad
who have celebrated 50-plus years of living happily ever after
and who continue to walk through life together still holding hands.
It is also dedicated to
my sister Marilyn and Hans
my niece Natasha and Blair
and
my niece Jasmine.

Acknowledgments

I WOULD LIKE to thank the talented team at Sourcebooks for their direction and guidance in the creation of *Your Stress-Free Wedding Planner*. It has been a great pleasure working with Deborah Werksman, whose support of my vision to present a wedding planner that would abate wedding planning anxiety and help couples to move forward with their wedding day plans with confidence and anticipation has been unwavering since day one. Deb's expertise and strength in producing books that meet the anticipated needs of those planning their weddings—books that are informative and educational—has been a guiding force in *Your Stress-Free Wedding Planner*.

Going through the process of copyediting and production of the manuscript with Kelly Barrales-Saylor has been effortless in her skilled hands and it has been a wonderful experience being able to work with her. Kelly is a true professional. Jenna Jakubowski, whose responsibilities include the cover and internal design, as well entering any edits once the book is laid out in pages, has done an outstanding job of capturing the wedding planner's essence and creating design that has great eye appeal. Morgan Hrejsa did a wonderful job of keeping everything and everyone on schedule. The coordination of the project between the acquiring editor, the copyediting and proofreading group, and the production department flowed with ease under her supervision. Jill Amack, who was responsible for doing the second read on the manuscript once it was in pages and assisted with the acquiring editor's focus group, was another key member of this amazing team led by Deb Werksman.

I would also like to thank Daphne Hart, my literary agent at Helen Heller Agency, Inc., who has shepherded me through five successful books, for bringing *Your Stress-Free Wedding Planner* to the attention of Deb Werksman and

Sourcebooks, Inc. It was, in a sense, a perfect marriage. Sourcebooks, Inc., is committed to producing books that will illuminate, inspire, enlighten, and have great value to their readers. Their intention is the exact match for what I want to bring forth by writing a wedding planner that would be educational and enlightening to couples setting out to plan one of the most special occasions in their lives. Thank you all for the important roles you played in producing this book.

About the Author

JUDY ALLEN IS a professional event planner and has created, produced, and flawlessly executed successful special events with up to 2,000 guests in more than thirty countries. The events she has done range from weddings to exclusive VIP social events and multimillion-dollar, multimedia corporate theme extravaganzas filled with special effects. The events Judy has designed and orchestrated include the opening theatrical gala for Disney for *Beauty and the Beast*, which was billed by the media as a "Beauty of a Bash" and the coordination of Oscar-Winning Director Norman Jewison's 25th Anniversary Celebration of *Fiddler on the Roof*.

One of the leading authorities on event planning, Allen is the author of four bestselling professional books on the subject:

- *Event Planning: The Ultimate Guide to Successful Meetings, Corporate Events, Fundraising Galas, Conferences, Conventions, Incentives and Other Special Events* (John Wiley & Sons, 2000)
- *The Business of Event Planning: Behind-the-Scenes Secrets of Successful Special Events* (John Wiley & Sons, 2002)
- *Event Planning: Ethics & Etiquette: A Principled Approach to the Business of Special Event Management* (John Wiley & Sons, 2003)
- *Marketing Your Event Planning Business: A Creative Approach to Gaining the Competitive Edge* (John Wiley & Sons, 2004).

She has also written an "Entertaining Ideas" column for the *New York Post's* PageSix.com, as well as feature articles and expert columns for magazines and newspapers.